Stress
Management

Richard Pettinger

Fast track route to mastering all aspects of stress
management

Covers all the key techniques for reducing stress in yourself
and your organization, from managing conflict to dealing with
bullying and discrimination, and from ensuring a safe physical
environment to improving labour relations

■ Examples and lessons from businesses that have successfully
tackled stress, including Nike, Sony and Semco Inc, and ideas
from the smartest thinkers, including Elaine Sternberg and
Charles Handy

■ Includes a glossary of key concepts and a comprehensive
resources guide

essential management thinking at your fingertips

LIFE & WORK

10.10

The right of Richard Pettinger to be identified as the author of this work has been asserted in accordance with the Copyright, Designs and Patents Act 1988

First published 2002 by
Capstone Publishing (A Wiley Company)
8 Newtec Place
Magdalen Road
Oxford OX4 1RE
United Kingdom
http://www.capstoneideas.com

CIP catalogue records for this book are available from the British Library and the US Library of Congress

ISBN 1-84112-319-6

Printed and bound in Great Britain

This book is printed on acid-free paper

Substantial discounts on bulk quantities of Capstone books are available to corporations, professional associations and other organizations. Please contact Capstone for more details on +44 (0)1865 798 623 or (fax) +44 (0)1865 240 941 or (e-mail) info@wiley-capstone.co.uk

Contents

Introduction to ExpressExec

ExpressExec is 3 million words of the latest management thinking compiled into 10 modules. Each module contains 10 individual titles forming a comprehensive resource of current business practice written by leading practitioners in their field. From brand management to balanced scorecard, ExpressExec enables you to grasp the key concepts behind each subject and implement the theory immediately. Each of the 100 titles is available in print and electronic formats.

Through the ExpressExec.com Website you will discover that you can access the complete resource in a number of ways:

» printed books or e-books;
» e-content – PDF or XML (for licensed syndication) adding value to an intranet or Internet site;
» a corporate e-learning/knowledge management solution providing a cost-effective platform for developing skills and sharing knowledge within an organization;
» bespoke delivery – tailored solutions to solve your need.

Why not visit www.expressexec.com and register for free key management briefings, a monthly newsletter and interactive skills checklists. Share your ideas about ExpressExec and your thoughts about business today.

Please contact elound@wiley-capstone.co.uk for more information.

Introduction to Stress Management

- » Costs
- » Human factors
- » Responsibilities
- » Conclusions

INTRODUCTION

Stress management is set to become a primary strategic and operational concern for all organizations because of the direct relationship between decency and humanity, good employment practice, and successful business. Stress places a cost burden on organizations in all locations and sectors, and there is also a human price among those who work in stressful situations or suffer from stress-related injuries and illnesses.

This is reinforced in the European Union (EU) by legislation that requires an active responsibility for the health and well-being of employees. It includes specific attention to stress. While this form of social workplace legislation is a lesser concern elsewhere, the costs of managing individual cases and situations are nevertheless high.

COSTS

Costs incurred include the following.

» The cost of having staff off sick for stress-related injuries and illness.
» The cost of paying compensation to those who can demonstrate and prove that their lives have been damaged or ruined as the result of stress at work.
» Costs in reputation and, invariably, business losses as the result of publicity surrounding specific media coverage in cases of accident, disaster, bullying, victimization, harassment and discrimination. These costs include customers taking business elsewhere when able to do so because no-one likes to be associated with this kind of organization. Such organizations experience increased difficulties in recruiting and retaining high quality, expert staff, because nobody with any choice in the matter wishes to work for such a concern.
» Organization and managerial costs involved in investing and defending individual and collective complaints of stress, and in remedying and resolving these.
» Costs involved in having to manage, address and resolve related issues, for example, where staff have turned to drink and drugs as a relief from stress.
» Wider humanitarian concerns that bring costs with them. Known, believed and perceived stress-related illnesses and injuries cause general damage to workplace and human morale and motivation.

HUMAN FACTORS

Some stress is physical, such as Repetitive Strain Injuries (RSIs) and back injuries, and therefore much easier to address both managerially and culturally. Problems are compounded, however, because so much stress is psychological and behavioral, and is therefore much more difficult to observe and quantify.

Stress also has a very strong subjective element. Some individuals take in their stride what others find extremely stressful. Some people find different parts of work more stressful than others. For example, some nurses regard having to do paperwork as an opportunity to sit down away from hospital ward pressures, while others resent it because it interferes with the ward work.

Some people complain of stress when, while it is known and understood that the particular working environment is very pressurized, this is nevertheless simply the norm for the particular occupation or organization. Those who do complain consequently come to be badly thought of, and so the individual pressure is compounded.

A major cause of individual stress is being on the receiving end of bullying, victimization, discrimination, and harassment. These activities are morally repugnant and an affront to basic humanity. They are endemic in all organizations, industrial, commercial, and public service sectors across the Western world and Far East. Organizations have active legal responsibilities in recognizing and resolving these matters in the EU, Australia, New Zealand and South Africa; and the moral and ethical case is absolute everywhere.

RESPONSIBILITIES

Effective stress management brings direct obligations and responsibilities, and these also have a cost. Organizations and their managers are going to be increasingly required to invest time, financial resources, and expertise in creating a quality of working life and environment that acknowledges the potential for stress. This requires recognizing where the potential for physical and psychological stress lies, and taking active steps in workplace, occupation and work design so that it is eliminated as far as possible, or else kept to a minimum. If this is not possible, organizations and their managers must be prepared to accept that they will face problems of absenteeism, illness, injury, and burnout as a result.

It is also essential to create managerial and supervisory styles that ensure that problems and issues are raised and dealt with early, rather than being allowed to fester (which is in itself stressful). The fundamental approach has to be based on openness, honesty, and integrity. It is essential that a mutual respect and value between staff and managers is created and developed. This is vital, and possible, regardless of whether the organization is hierarchical, bureaucratic, authoritarian, participative or democratic.

A general climate of mutual confidence is also required. This enables all those involved to talk openly about problems and issues so that they can be raised at whatever stage they become apparent, and from whatever source. This includes providing the capacity and willingness to address serious problems – especially those raised by "whistle-blowers."

An active management engagement is required in recognizing the institutional sources, causes, and potential for individual and collective conflict. This means acknowledging that the potential for conflict exists in all human situations, and this includes places of work. Managers are increasingly required to assess their own organizations, those employed, and desired and required ways of working, from the point of view of recognizing the potential for conflict in the particular situation. They are also required to create and develop the conditions in which conflict can be kept to a minimum and resolved quickly when it does break out. See Summary box 1.1 for examples.

SUMMARY BOX 1.1: STRESS AT WORK: INITIAL EXAMPLES

The need to recognize and address the relationship between particular occupational, professional, and work patterns and stress and conflict is present in all industries and occupations. Here are some examples.

» **Hospitals**: it is impossible for anyone to deliver sustained and effective long-term performance if they are working a prescribed working week of 72 hours (6 x 12 hour shifts as with UK junior hospital doctors). Indeed, some junior hospital doctors in the UK effectively work, or are on-call, the full 168 hours per week.

» **Financial services**: financial services and investment management in Japan also adopt these "long hours" cultures. Some big banks require that all their staff arrive before the local senior manager or chief executive and do not leave until he does. Hundreds of staff consequently find themselves sleeping at the office for several days at a time.

» **Football**: professional footballers in Italy do not work under such pressure, however their only genuinely free time is between the end of matches at approximately 5.00pm on Sundays and bedtime that evening. Every other hour of the week is organized on behalf of the players by the clubs. Serious stress is caused if, for any reason, the players are not allowed out at this time. This is in spite of the fact that extremely high salary levels are paid (up to $400,000 per week in many instances).

CONCLUSIONS

Initially therefore, it is essential to understand the extent and prevalence of stress. While it is clearly understood to be a problem in some sectors, occupations, and professions, it should be recognized that stress has the potential to exist – and indeed does exist – across all sectors, industries, and national and social cultures. It is essential that organizations, managers, and individuals understand the costs that are attached to it, and the benefits of understanding, recognizing, and addressing stress successfully and effectively.

What is Stress Management?

» Understanding stress
» Stress and work
» Conclusions

INTRODUCTION

Effective stress management is concerned with:

» understanding stress, its sources, causes, symptoms and results;
» designing the work environment and different aspects of organization and workplace practice so that the effect of stress can be minimized;
» creating the conditions in which specific issues can be dealt with quickly when they become apparent; and
» recognizing the interaction between life at work, and that outside work; and taking steps to understand the stresses and strains thus caused (this is currently the subject of legislation in the EU, and certain to be a social/occupational legal issue in North America).

UNDERSTANDING STRESS

Stress is placed on anything that is given special emphasis or significance, especially where this leads to, or involves, psychological, emotional, and physical strain or tension. A part of it is therefore subjective, in that different reactions are produced in different individuals by the same set of circumstances. Stress is caused by a combined physical and psychological response to stimuli (stressors) that occur or are encountered during the course of living.

Cooper (1997)[1] summarizes stress as:

"everything that deprives the person of purpose and zest, that leaves him with negative feelings about himself, with anxieties, tensions, a sense of lostness, emptiness and futility."

Fontana (1989)[2] draws the meaning of the word from the Latin *stringere*, meaning "to draw tight," and from the French word *destresse*, meaning "to be placed under narrowness or oppression."

Statt (1994)[3] draws attention to the physical response:

"the human body is biologically programmed to react to challenges from the environment by mobilizing its resources. We can either confront the challenge and fight it or get away from it as fast as possible. The choice in other words is "fight or flight", whichever we deem to be more appropriate in the situation. If our brain perceives an imminent challenge, the message it passes to our autonomic nervous system results immediately in the hormones adrenaline and noradrenaline being released into the bloodstream where they speed up our reflexes, raise the level of blood sugar and increase our blood pressure and heart rate. The digestive system closes down allowing the blood used in the normal process of digesting food to be re-routed to the muscles and lungs. Endorphins are released into the bloodstream, which reduce pain and sensitivity to bruising and injury. Cortisone is released from the adrenal glands into the bloodstream, which slows the body's immune system. Finally, the blood vessels constrict while the blood thickens, flows more slowly, and coagulates more quickly. The sum of these changes is to prepare us to deal with a short-term emergency situation. Stress occurs when these physiological reactions cannot deal with the environmental challenge.''

STRESS AND WORK

In spite of the fact that stress is an individual reaction, it is important to recognize that certain organizational, occupational, environmental, and managerial conditions are much more likely to produce adverse human reactions. Key concerns are:

» work and occupational conditions and environment;
» specific problems, including RSI, and the extent and prevalence of bullying, victimization, discrimination and harassment;
» role conflicts;
» organization structure and culture; and
» workplace relationships.

Work and occupational conditions and the environment

Arnold (1997)[4] identified five key elements relating to job stress as follows:

» making decisions;
» constant monitoring of devices or materials;
» repeated exchange of information with others;

» unpleasant physical conditions; and
» performing unstructured, rather than structured, tasks.

The greater the extent to which any job, profession or occupation possesses each of these elements, the higher is the general level of stress. While it is possible to reduce or minimize the effects of stress where one or two of these conditions are prevalent, it is not easy where all five are present. To these may be added the following:

» resources, expertise, and other staff and equipment shortages;
» uncertainty of tenure;
» adversarial or dishonest managerial and supervisory styles and approaches; and
» lack of known, believed, and perceived adequate intrinsic and extrinsic rewards.

It is likely that some of these will also be present to an extent in most occupations. However, it is the extent and mix of each that causes occupational stress. Problems are compounded when those in known or believed stressful situations and occupations understand that they are being overloaded with work when others elsewhere in the particular organization are not.

This may or may not be true. It does indicate the prime importance of an open and visible managerial style as a prerequisite to the effective recognition and acceptance of stress caused by problems at work. If it is impossible to raise or observe such matters, it is extremely hard for there to be any effective subsequent action.

Specific problems

Stress is caused when bullying, victimization, harassment, and discrimination occur and are allowed to persist. It is also a serious problem when an individual comes across an aspect of organizational or occupational malpractice and feels powerless to do anything about it. Each of these stems from the illegitimate use of power by individuals, groups or the organization as a whole based on:

» position, rank and status;
» resource command and control; and
» physical power, strength, and size.

The most common outputs are:

» sexual harassment, usually of female staff by males;
» threatening behavioral and physical violence towards an individual or group; and
» threatening attitudes and behavior towards subordinates by seniors involving the misuse and abuse of disciplinary and poor performance procedures; and in many cases, this is compounded still by adversarial general attitudes that may be summarized as: "If you do not do this work or want this job, there are millions out there who do."

Roles

Roles are combinations of behavior and activities undertaken by people in different sets of circumstances. Everyone performs a great variety of roles during their lives (see Figure 2.1). Each role has expectations, pressures, rewards, and consequences. There are overlaps between each and measures of honesty, discord, and conflict.

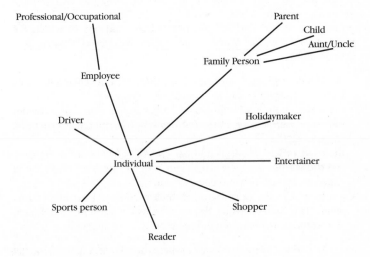

Fig. 2.1 Individual roles.

Stress is caused where there are role uncertainties and ambiguities, role overlap (especially between work and non-work), role incompatibility, and role overload and underload. Each of these elements is dealt with extensively in Chapter 6.

Organization culture

Organization culture is the summary of attitudes, values, beliefs, and activities carried out. Often summarized as "the way things are done here," it is a combination of:

» the origins, history, and traditions of the organization;
» its strategy and policies;
» the nature of its activities;
» the relationship between technology and the workforce, work design, organization, and structure; and
» levels of stability and change.

Culture is reinforced by the stated and actual purposes, priorities and attention given to performance, staff, customers, suppliers, the community, and the environment, and to progress and development.

Creating an effective and positive culture, and one in which the presence and potential of stress can be acknowledged and managed, is dependent on:

» the extent to which dominant values, attitudes, and beliefs advocated by the organizations can gain universal acceptance;
» the nature of the philosophy of the organization, especially whether this is precise, positive, and stated, or allowed to emerge unstructured and undirected;
» the ways in which norms and patterns of behavior are developed, and the reasons for these; and again, whether they are positive and engaging, or negative and coercive; and
» the climate of the organization, which is conveyed by the environment, the physical layout, the ways in which participants interact, and relationships between different levels in the hierarchy.

Stress in working relations is caused where there is a lack of fundamental identity or cohesion from any of these points of view. In these cases, staff groups retreat into themselves. Their loyalties become tainted and divided. High status, professional, and expert groups identify with each other rather than with their organization, and this leads to the formation of *canteen* cultures and *bunker* mentalities (see Summary box 2.1).

SUMMARY BOX 2.1: CANTEEN CULTURES AND BUNKER MENTALITIES AS A SOURCE OF STRESS

This is a serious problem in many organizations, locations, and sectors. Here is an example.

Japanese government emergency response

The inadequacy of the Japanese government in responding quickly to crises and emergencies became apparent at the time of the Japanese Airlines disaster of 1987 and the Kobe earthquake of 1992. There was a direct conflict between the need to respond quickly, the capability to do this, and the perceived political drive of cabinet ministers and senior public officials. The need to respond quickly was driven by the fact that in each case a speedy response would save lives. The capability was present – but it was not Japanese. It was American.

US military personnel stationed in Japan and trained in disaster management and rescue missions were on both occasions capable and available. They were not called on because of the perceived loss of face that would have arisen if the government, by implication, was seen to be unable to respond to its own crises and emergencies.

Considerable stress was therefore caused all round. US military personnel were forced to stand by and watch people die or become seriously ill. Those involved in the crises and their relatives would have accepted help from anywhere. Senior Japanese political and public figures acknowledged the problems, but because of their own cultural pressures were nevertheless required to tackle them in their own ways. This is not a judgment on what was done, or on why or how it was done. It does, however, illustrate the extensive potential for cultural differences and working relations and the resulting clashes that can lead to stress.

Working relations

Effective working relations are based on a fundamental openness and transparency of organizational and managerial approach and style. This is reinforced by a strong, positive, designed, and cohesive organization culture capable of universal acceptance. It is also required that a known and understood mutuality of interest, that transcends occupational and professional groups and vested interests, is present. This must be capable of addressing and resolving role and other conflicts whenever they become apparent. This is referred to in Chapters 4 and 5, and discussed fully in Chapter 6.

CONCLUSIONS

Some occupations are inherently more stressful than others, and some organizations much more stressful places in which to work than others. It is useful to illustrate the kinds of jobs that, all things being equal, are more and less stressful than others (see Table 2.1).

It is clear that many of these are generic job titles, rather than specific occupational descriptions. However, it does indicate the inherent extent and potential for stress when individuals and groups with different expertise are employed. The nature of work, and the context in which it is required to be carried out, can therefore be addressed from a much greater level of general understanding, and as a precursor to developing specific remedies.

KEY LEARNING POINTS

» Stress is an individual, as well as a predictable, reaction to stimuli and challenges.
» Stress is a combined physical and psychological reaction; and it carries negative, rather than positive, connotations.
» Stress is caused universally by fundamental affronts to humanity, especially bullying, victimization, harassment, and discrimination.
» The effective management of stress at work requires attention to the working environment, individual roles, and functions, and understanding the potential for conflict.

Table 2.1 Occupational stress scale.

Miner	8.3	Farmer	4.8
Police	7.7	Armed Forces	4.7
Construction worker	7.5	Vet	4.5
Journalist	7.5	Civil servant	4.4
Pilot (civil)	7.5	Accountant	4.3
Prison officer	7.5	Engineer	4.3
Advertising	7.3	Estate agent	4.3
Dentist	7.3	Hairdresser	4.3
Actor	7.2	Local government officer	4.3
Politician	7.0	Secretary	4.3
Doctor	6.8	Solicitor	4.3
Taxman	6.8	Artist, designer	4.0
Film producer	6.5	Architect	4.0
Nurse, midwife	6.5	Chiropodist	4.0
Fireman	6.3	Optician	4.0
Musician	6.3	Planner	4.0
Teacher	6.2	Postman	4.0
Personnel	6.0	Statistician	4.0
Social worker	6.0	Lab technician	3.8
Manager (commercial)	5.8	Banker	3.7
Marketing (export)	5.8	Computing	3.7
Press officer	5.8	Occupational therapist	3.7
Professional footballer	5.8	Linguist	3.7
Salesperson, shop assistant	5.7	Beauty therapist	3.5
Stockbroker	5.5	Priest	3.5
Bus driver	5.4	Astronomer	3.4
Psychologist	5.2	Nursery nurse	3.3
Publishing	5.0	Museum worker	2.8
Diplomat	4.8	Librarian	2.0

Source: Statt, D.A. (1994)

NOTES

1 Cooper, G. (1997) *Managing Stress*. John Wiley.
2 Fontana, D. (1989) *Managing Stress*. Routledge.
3 Statt, D. (1994) *Psychology and the World of Work*. Macmillan.
4 Arnold, J. (1997) *Work Psychology*. Pitman.

Evolution of Stress and Stress Management

» Shell shock
» Scientific management
» Costs
» Conclusions

INTRODUCTION

It is apparent from social history studies that a great deal of life and occupational stress existed for centuries before it became acknowledged as such. For example:

» under the feudal system, serfs lived or died at the whim of their landlords;

» the price of failure in military campaigns, for foot-soldiers at least, was normally death; and

» the first factories of the Industrial Revolution offered a form of Hobson's choice – to work and live in the dreadful urban conditions of the eighteenth and nineteenth centuries, or not to work (and therefore live) at all.

SHELL SHOCK

The first identification of stress as an occupational factor and hazard arose during World War I (1914–1918). A direct relationship was identified between prolonged exposure to military engagement and the resulting loss of sight, hearing, orientation, and reason. This was defined as "shell shock." It was often accompanied by physical loss of strength and sickness, and compounded by revulsion at the conditions in the trenches.

SCIENTIFIC MANAGEMENT

Also at the beginning of the twentieth century, the first stress-related problems with production line factory work were identified. F.W. Taylor and the Scientific Management School designed factory work so that it consisted of a simple series of repetitive tasks in which individuals would soon become expert and proficient. They reasoned that so long as high levels of wages were paid, this form of work would be satisfactory and desirable. However, they failed to realize the levels of stress generated by excessive noise and dust, extremes of heat and cold, and the physical monotony of the work. Moreover, because there was no other challenge or content to the work, production line staff began to suffer psychological as well as physical health problems.

Affluent workers

This was seen again in the "Affluent Worker" studies of the 1950s. These studies were carried out in the UK at car engineering and chemical factories. They identified high collective stress levels in production staff. This was reinforced by a lack of identity between workers and the company, and any social interaction at the place of work. The concept of workplace and workforce alienation was born – a lack of any interest or commitment on the part of staff to company, or vice versa, except for the wage-work bargain. This level of stress was only sustainable so long as wages remained high, quality and volume of output remained low, and was not subject to managerial pressure. The management of stress was reinforced from time to time with 'safety-valving' by which staff, trade unions, and managers effectively conspired to engineer strikes of several days' or even weeks' duration in order to reduce stress levels and give everyone a break from the situation.

The other contribution of scientific management and "Affluent Worker" studies was to make clear that stress was suffered by everyone placed in bad working conditions and required to work to patterns over which they had little or no control. This has become a substantial contribution to the understanding of stress in overtly high value, professional, and expert occupations also, and provides a key point for organizational and managerial intervention.

Police studies

A further contribution to overall understanding was made by the United States Police Service studies of the 1970s. These addressed general levels of stress, as well as the specific issues of conformity, belonging, and identity. They were carried out in New York City, Ohio, and California.

A key finding was the pressure on police officers to conform to, or at least connive at, criminal activities, and to take rewards from those. This caused extreme stress to many individuals. Almost everyone had originally come into the service to serve the community. Yet here they were being pressured by their peers to become involved in exactly those activities that they were supposed to be stamping out. Many staff were driven out of the service altogether, while many others retired on health grounds.

Personality types

In the 1970s and 1980s, key medical research was linking behavior (including organizational behavior and the behavior of individuals at work) with stress, and identified heart disease as a major output of prolonged endurance of high levels of stress. These studies identified two personality types, which they called *Type A* and *Type B*.

Type As were identified as being action and results oriented, and in a hurry to complete work and move on to the next task. *Type As* tended to work faster and harder than *Type Bs*.

Type Bs were identified as being calm and unruffled. They rarely demonstrated high levels of emotion even in a crisis or emergency.

However, it is important to note that:

» *Type As* tended towards work and occupational overload. They were much more likely to take on too much work. They exhibited greater signs of stress. They were much more likely to experience conflict and to become sidetracked into non-essential tasks and activities. While they overtly worked harder than *Type Bs*, they were not necessarily as effective. Also, it became apparent that effort alone did not always bring additional rewards or promotions. Moreover, for *Type As* other opportunities were limited, except in terms of expanding and extending their existing job or position.

» *Type Bs* tended to reach the most senior positions in organizations. This was because they were calmer, and more ordered and strategic in approach. They did not confuse action and energy expenditure with effectiveness. They were also found to be much less prone to loss of reputation through open engagement in conflict; or more seriously, occupational and other health problems such as coronary heart disease.

The studies also found that *Type A* managers were much more likely to smoke, and to have higher blood pressure and cholesterol levels than *Type Bs*.

However, it is clear that both types have advantages and shortcomings. *Type As* tend to excel on tasks that have to be completed under time and resource pressures, and to become impatient with those who block them or hold them up. They exhibit ambition, drive, enthusiasm, and commitment. They also clearly expect and anticipate promotions,

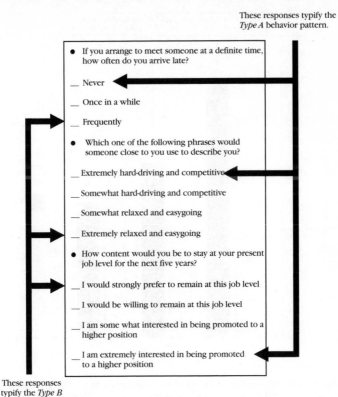

These responses typify the *Type A* behavior pattern.

- If you arrange to meet someone at a definite time, how often do you arrive late?

__ Never

__ Once in a while

__ Frequently

- Which one of the following phrases would someone close to you use to describe you?

__ Extremely hard-driving and competitive

__ Somewhat hard-driving and competitive

__ Somewhat relaxed and easygoing

__ Extremely relaxed and easygoing

- How content would you be to stay at your present job level for the next five years?

__ I would strongly prefer to remain at this job level

__ I would be willing to remain at this job level

__ I am some what interested in being promoted to a higher position

__ I am extremely interested in being promoted to a higher position

These responses typify the *Type B* behavior pattern

Fig. 3.1 Measuring the *Type A* and *Type B* behavior patterns: an example.

advancements, and rewards whether or not these are forthcoming (see Figure 3.1).

Type Bs tend to excel where a more considered approach is required. This especially means attention to the quality of results and output – the right answer at the deadline, not just any answer. Also in spite of the stated ambition drive, *Type Bs* tend to make it to the very top, even though *Type As* change their jobs much more frequently.

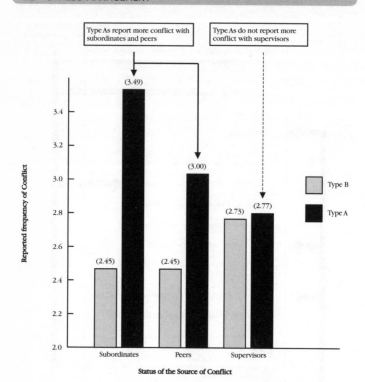

Fig. 3.2 Conflict and the *Type A* behavior pattern. **Source**: Greenberg, J. and Baron, R.A. (1995) *Behavior in Organizations*. Prentice Hall International.

Personality type and conflict

As stated above, *Type As* are much more likely to experience and become involved in conflict (see Figure 3.2).

Subsequent research (Baron, 1987)[1] conducted in the food industry again found that *Type As* were much more likely to engage in conflicts with subordinates and peers. There was, however, little difference when it came to engaging in open conflict with superiors. This indicates the following.

» The need for organizations and their managers to pay attention to personality, as well as profession and occupation, in the management of groups. Problems clearly arise when individuals are seen only as highly active, extremely busy or high achievers in terms of their output volume alone. It is necessary to attend to ways of working so that the high levels of commitment, energy, and capability brought by *Type As* result in excellent performance output without the attendant conflict-induced stress (see Summary box 3.1).

» The need for organizations and their managers to fully understand the costs and benefits of allowing these ways of working to continue. In terms of individual output, the contribution of *Type As* is very high. In terms of stress and conflict caused in dealings with others, much of the effectiveness of this contribution is likely to be dissipated in paying for organizational and managerial time, effort, and resources required for the resolution of disputes and grievances in the wake of the progress of the high achiever.

» It also implies an ethical responsibility to ensure that conditions are created so that *Type As* can work effectively at their professions, occupation or expertise by setting collective standards of attitude, behavior, and performance to which everyone can conform. These are then reinforced with effective performance appraisal that identifies organizational and occupational development needs so that *Type As* are enhanced by directing their energies into productive and effective output only.

These studies are a major contribution to understanding stress at work in that they relate behavior, drives, personality, and occupation. There are also specific management interventions clearly indicated.

SUMMARY BOX 3.1: GETTING TO THE VERY TOP

This helps to explain why so many high achieving and self-evidently excellent professional and occupational performers do not make good directors, and where the organization and managerial interventions required to get over this should actually be made.

This is a problem in public services, and industry and commerce. It indicates that subject teaching and learning in the areas of personality, understanding, management, and self-understanding are required for the effective transformation of excellent professional and occupational achievers into top managers. The present finding is that, because these subjects are not addressed, such persons (especially *Type As*) tend to rely on the qualities that have got them so far to take them on further still. It is also likely that *Type Bs* are much more receptive to the fact that the skills, qualities, and expertise that have got them so far will no longer be adequate if there is to be further progress. This has direct implications for training and development for top jobs.

» In public professions such as nursing, teaching, and social services work, frontline work requires the energy, commitment, enthusiasm, and dynamism of *Type As*; but managing, ordering, and directing these professions requires the calm and considered strategy approach of *Type Bs*. Failure to recognize and understand this means that there are always going to be skills and experience gaps if *Type As* are promoted.
» In industrial and commercial professions such as sales and marketing, again the frontline is highly results orientated and driven; and again where the strategic approach is required, shortfalls become apparent.

In both cases, the problem is compounded because higher pay and reward levels are almost universally given to managers rather than those at the frontline. Therefore, anyone who needs or wants increased recognition and rewards is pressurized into applying for jobs that they are likely to be unable to do.

Recent studies

Recent studies have tended to concentrate on different aspects of stress management. At both macro and micro levels they have looked at how to reduce stress levels in working environments and also at the human and economic costs incurred.

Goodness of fit

Furnham and Schaeffer (1984)[2] proposed the concept of "goodness of fit" between individuals, their organization, and their occupation. This reinforced the subjectivity of stress – the fact that one person's stress is another's interest, stimulus or indifference. The key is to ensure that individual professions and occupations provide the "right amount" of stimulation, creativity, drive, reward, challenge, and progress. Where these are out of harmony with each other, symptoms of stress such as frustration, conflict, dispute, and other behavioral and attitudinal problems are likely to occur. This again reinforces the need to understand stress as a key aspect of management knowledge and expertise.

Karoushi

Tubbs (1993)[3] identified Karoushi or "stress death" during studies of patterns of work in large corporations in Japan. The original hypothesis was that the sheer physical and psychological demands of working long hours every day meant that people were dying of exhaustion.

Tubbs found however that the killer – the last straw – was stress. People who worked long hours felt that they had to and that they had no control over their working lives or the demands placed on them by their employers. Many depended on the overtime to make ends meet, to provide for wives and children, and to ensure social standing. It was these pressures that caused death, not the long hours themselves.

COSTS

The costs of stress to employers, as well as employees, have never been fully or completely calculated. However, a variety of individual studies and statistics give a clear indication.

A UK labor research department report published in 1983 stated that there were then three million excessive drinkers in England and Wales, and 850,000 problem and dependent drinkers. About one in twenty-five of the population in England and Wales, and possibly as high as one in ten in Scotland, may be personally affected by severe alcohol-related problems.

A survey by Canada Health Monitor (2000) found that 25% of workers reported stress, psychological or emotional problems arising from work (as opposed to 9% who said that they suffered from workplace injury, and 9% who said they suffered from illness brought on by bad working conditions, noise, dust, heat, and cold). It was estimated that the cost of stress to Canadian industry, commerce, and public services was in the order of Can$300,000,000,000 per annum.

CONCLUSIONS

It is clear that key contributions to understanding what stress is, and its effects on people at work, have been made from many different sources. The body of knowledge and experience on which effective stress management is based addresses the outputs, costs, and consequences, as well as understanding the physical, behavioral, and psychological aspects. It is essential that managers take time to understand and become aware of the subject from the broadest possible point of view. Then, whether or not the problem is institutionally recognized, at least individual managers and those who work for them have a much greater understanding of what is likely to occur in their own domain, and can begin to take effective steps to address the issues.

KEY LEARNING POINTS

» The identification of stress in many different environments.
» The relationship between personality and stress.
» Problems and issues in personality management.
» Problems and issues in the management of promotion and opportunity.
» The relationship between stress and different patterns of work.
» The costs of stress.

NOTES

1 Baron, R.A. (1987) *Behavior in Organizations*. Allyn and Bacon.
2 Furnham, A. & Schaeffer, R. (1984) "Job satisfaction and mental health." *Journal of Occupational Psychology*, 57, 295–305.
3 Tubbs, W. (1993) "Stress death." *Journal of Business Ethics*, 12, 859–77.

The E-Dimension

» Work structure and environment
» Communications and information
» E-markets
» Management and supervisory style
» Use and value of technology
» Conclusions
» Best practice casestudy: Tescodirect.com

INTRODUCTION

The Internet, e-business and e-communications have implications for the management of stress in the following areas:

» work structure and environment;
» communications and information;
» markets;
» management, supervisory style, and attitudes; and
» use and value of the technology.

WORK STRUCTURE AND ENVIRONMENT

For many organizations, professions, and occupations, the Internet has brought great benefits. These include:

» the speed and ability to communicate with everybody (and to receive communications);
» the provision of standard bodies of information quickly and effectively; and
» the ability to support organization and employee development initiatives with Website materials and interactive exercises.

It is also an effective means of keeping staff records and bodies of organizational knowledge, experience, and expertise, which can be accessed by those who are given passwords.

At its most effective, the e-dimension has brought high levels of support for strategic, operational, and functional management working in all sectors. Additional benefits are apparent for large, complex, and diversified organizations, and those with staff and activities in remote parts of the world.

The problems related to stress arise as follows.

» If e-mail and the Internet are used as the only, or major, form of communication, then this reinforces rather than dissipates feelings of isolation on the part of staff working in remote locations or away from head office. This leads to feelings of helplessness, loss of control, and the absence of known and perceived points of reference. Conducted in isolation, e-mail contacts and Web-based information systems give no indication of the inflections or nuances of what is being said, why or how, and little of the attitudes and expectations of those sending the communication (see Summary box 4.1).

SUMMARY BOX 4.1: SHORTFALLS IN E-MAIL AND E-COMMUNICATION

Consider the following note. It was sent to a young computer project engineer who was working in Hanoi, Vietnam, by his boss who was in Los Angeles.

> "We have heard nothing from you for three weeks. We do not know whether all is going well or not. Above all, is the project launched? Has it started well? Above all, are there any teething troubles? That's what I want to know."

The range of reactions can be anything from assertive and straightforward to serious stress. Stress is compounded if additional contact is not available by telephone or face to face with local organization representatives and staff.

Stress may also be caused by working for two bosses in such situations. Commands issued by e-mail from head office, and face to face from the organization's local or regional manager, may be directly contrary, or give different inflections and nuances.

The note above also gives no idea of the state of mind of the sender – whether anxious, angry, concerned or upset; whether the requests are being made because he/she wants to know, or because he/she has been asked to find out by someone else; or whether it is indeed a straightforward professional and concerned note.

So effective work structure and environment requires universal understanding that the Web and e-mail systems are for the support and enhancement of what is done, and are not a substitute.

» Some organizations are also considering the possibility of using the Web for personality tests, performance appraisals, and the management of grievances and disputes. It is possible that such approaches may speed up and enhance the operation of these matters. However, they must always be followed up, confirmed, and conducted in substance face to face. Conducted in isolation, to "fail" the personality test (e.g. as part of the assessment process for promotion, or for assessing trainability and aptitude) without a visible debrief is certain to cause resentment and frustration. To receive the outcome of a grievance or dispute by e-mail is satisfactory only if the employee's case is settled entirely in their favor; otherwise again, stress is certain to result. It is very difficult to see how any effective performance appraisal could be carried out by e-mail except at the initial stage of a particular process where manager and subordinate exchange notes concerning their view of progress to date and over the period, as a precursor to a face-to-face discussion.

» The physical structure of the work also needs to be considered. Internet-based activities and occupations require workstations that are functionally effective, and also of a good human quality. Poor quality and badly designed working environments in factory and production line work have also been proven and demonstrated to cause stress and illness (see Chapters 2 and 3) and this also applies to computer-based activities. Working in cubicles, staring at screens, and being subjected to confrontational and adversarial managers and supervisors is certain to produce the same feelings of frustration, lack of value, helplessness – and stress – as in traditional industrial situations.

COMMUNICATIONS AND INFORMATION

The Internet and e-mail systems are potentially excellent sources of communications and information providing quick and easy access for all. Problems arise when some, or all, of the following conditions exist.

Information overload

Information overload occurs when people are sent, or are required to access, too much information for them to be able to assimilate. This is often due to a lack of understanding or empathy. For example, while it may be convenient to *send* a 100-page report by e-mail, it is not always convenient to *receive* it that way, because it has either to be read off the screen, or else printed off first.

"All-staffers"

"All staff" e-mails are a nuisance (if not a primary stressor) especially when the receivers have plenty of other things to do, because they have to be read before it is apparent whether they have any direct value or priority.

Problems are reinforced in large, complex corporations when it is known, believed or perceived that "all-staffers" are being sent out either to justify someone's existence, or as a realpolitik marketing exercise (see Summary box 4.2).

SUMMARY BOX 4.2: INFORMATION OVERLOAD

One of the UK's top universities created an information systems division. This was funded partly from central government. In addition, it received a foundation grant and subsidized hardware and software. Consisting of 20 staff, it was to be paid for on a continuing basis by "top slicing" – a levy on each of the academic teaching and research departments of the university.

This caused initial resentment among heads of faculty and departments because it was widely believed that the university had created the division because it felt that it ought to have one, rather than because there was a known and understood operational demand.

This perception was reinforced when, after three months of operations, it became apparent that the new information systems division was producing 98% of "all-staffers" and 21% of all e-mails. Shortly afterwards, the information systems division had its remit extended to cover security and internal hardware and software purchasing and management. This caused extensive disruption to existing administrative functions and purchasing procedures, all of which were clearly known and understood. The impression left was that this was an expensive exercise that had to be paid for out of primary activities – teaching and research – and that, rather than admitting a mistake and canceling the project, something now had to be found for the new department to do.

Information underload

This occurs where:

» staff are not getting sufficient information;
» staff are not getting the information that they need and want;
» staff are not getting it in the right format, so while the volume of information may be overload, its quality, value, and usefulness are not suitable; and
» not all staff are getting information, usually because of organization realpolitik in which information is rationed on a "need to know" approach based on status and exclusivity rather than operational demand; or because not all staff have access to information systems.

This last is especially a problem with junior, frontline, and operational staff in all parts of industry, commerce, and public services who complain that they never get to hear of policy and operational decisions that they are expected to implement because the information is communicated electronically to their superiors, and then edited or skewed versions are subsequently issued by edict.

Underload also reinforces other stressors that may be present. This especially refers to differentials based on status, role, and hierarchical advantages and disadvantages; and beliefs and perceptions that frontline staff are being overloaded to compensate for strategic and operational blunders or status-based enhancements (see Summary box 4.3).

SUMMARY BOX 4.3: INFORMATION UNDERLOAD

A survey conducted in the UK in February 2001 found that part of the reason for information underload, and a lack of adequate information being transmitted to frontline staff, was that managers, supervisors, and bureaucrats did not know how to do this electronically. Rather than find out and become proficient in the use of information systems, they simply failed to pass on the information.

Feelings of frustration were compounded by another finding, which stated that the UK's managers spent an average of three hours per week surfing the Internet looking for matters of general interest, pursuing hobbies and interests, and booking holidays. Many would also try to make business travel bookings. Attention was especially drawn to this last point because the overwhelming majority of organizations have institutional booking systems that are effectively managed by clerical and support functions.

The survey concluded that for many managers, computers were little more than corporate toys, appendages or playthings. It was very difficult to understand what discernible strategic and operational advantages had accrued as the result of the almost universal distribution of personal computers to functional and operational managers.

Source: Office Angels Employment Services Group Plc., web@Work Survey (2001).

Security

The security of electronic mail and information systems is a problem when it is known, believed or perceived that personal data may be available to people other than those who have a legitimate interest and access to it. Of especial importance are:

» problems surrounding personnel and human resource management information held on organizational databases that may be accessed for non-legitimate reasons and/or by those who have no legitimate business doing so; and
» financial problems caused by known and perceived capabilities in accessing personal banking and financial information, and credit card details.

It is therefore essential to understand that those responsible for securing the quality and confidentiality of information may have to be able to demonstrate this from time to time. In the EU, employees have statutory rights concerning access to data held in electronic filing systems, and this is required by law to be both accurate and verifiable, and also accessible at all times by the individual concerned.

E-MARKETS

Stress on the commercial and operational front has been generated for the following reasons.

» Fashionable and faddish drives to create Websites, interactive, and virtual facilities on which there are envisaged standard commercial returns.
» High levels of investment either placed with dot.com entrepreneurs or by traditional companies in Website ventures on which standard commercial returns are also envisaged and required.
» Drives to produce Websites in spite of a lack of full understanding of the relationship between Website production and enhanced performance; and compounded by a lack of clarity surrounding the contribution made to strategy, marketing, products and service delivery, and financial performance.
» Lack of results on e-ventures (see Summary box 4.4). Part of this is due to a lack of understanding of the results that such ventures can be expected to produce. This has been compounded by the fashion/faddish drive indicated above. Part is attributable to wider losses of confidence on the NASDAQ, the hi-tech stock market.

Part is also attributable to a collective and individual unwillingness to try to establish what is possible and what is not. While levels and rates of return on investments in cars, carpets, bricks, and airlines are well known, those on e-ventures are not. Neither have organizations, or their managers, been willing to admit that they do not know this, and consequently little has been done about it.

SUMMARY BOX 4.4: PRODUCING RESULTS IN E-VENTURES

It is possible to produce positive results. There are many successful e-ventures, especially in the provision of industrial marketing and business products and services. There is also plenty of evidence that Web-based activities make a valuable and effective contribution provided that they are fully integrated with the physical and traditional elements. The following is an example.

Ryan Air
The Irish low-budget airline provides all of its brochures, time-tables and range of ancillary services (car hire, hotel bookings) on-line. This is supported with fully serviced customer and client helplines to which ready and immediate access is always possible. There are very few instances of having to queue on the telephone in order to confirm bookings or speak to the company's customer services section. This, in turn, is reinforced by the clear standards and values of the company's owner, Michael O'Leary.

Mr O'Leary understands that stress is caused:

» to customers when they cannot easily make bookings or gain ready access to staff, making them likely to take their business elsewhere; and
» to staff, as the result of having to field large volumes of negative attitudes from customers.

He has therefore taken all possible steps to ensure that his company removes these two main causes of stress (and loss of business performance).

MANAGEMENT AND SUPERVISORY STYLE

The response of organizations, and their managers and supervisors, has crossed the entire range of management styles in the search to resolve stresses and strains caused by the e-dimension. The following are examples.

» **Boo.com:** the Swedish Internet footwear retailer adopted a fully participative and involved management style. Employees were allowed to set their own hours and patterns of work subject only to product and service delivery. They could dress as they pleased. A high quality of working comfort, environment, and life was assured.

Most of the stressors found elsewhere were removed. The company foundered on the lack of viability of the strategic business proposition. There were simply insufficient customers who were prepared to buy their shoes on-line.

» **Semco**: the Brazilian engineering and white goods manufacturer has developed its e-business as the sales and service point for its existing range of activities, and as a fund of expertise available on a consultancy basis to anyone who would like it. The company is fully participative (see Chapter 7). Like Boo.com, the company allows all staff to set their own hours of work. Staff also set their own salaries, and can choose to work as subcontractors rather than employees if they so wish. All employees have, and are required to take, six weeks' holiday per annum. The company's management and organization style has the express purpose of removing all sources of stress and strain from the place of work. Indeed, the primary reason for adopting the approach was because traditional ways of working had brought the company chief executive officer, Ricardo Semler, to what his doctor described as "the most advanced case of stress I have ever seen in anyone of your age."

» **A survey** published by the UK Institute of Management in February 2000 found that e-mails were a contribution to high levels of stress. Conducted overwhelmingly among line, functional, and divisional managers it found that early optimism about technological advance had brought additional burdens and increased work pressures.

The key to all effective management and supervisory styles is a combination of integrity, respect, openness, visibility, and enthusiasm. This is combined with a full understanding of the activities for which managers are responsible, what is required, how and why, and the environmental pressures in which they are conducted.

From this point of view, the key to effective management of the hi-tech and e-dimensions of stress requires the same basic approach. Understanding the capabilities and constraints of the technology, and the circumstances under which it is to be used, are primary active managerial requirements. Unless this is achieved, effectiveness of usage is always diluted. This results in additional stresses and strains on staff. The consequence is that the e-dimension itself becomes a source of dispute, grievance, poor and declining performance, and additional managerial and operational pressures.

USE AND VALUE OF TECHNOLOGY

The critical issue in managing stress in the e-dimension is understanding the use and value of the technology. This means understanding its overall capability and capacity, understanding the purposes for which the organization specifically requires it, and addressing discrepancies between the two.

It is consequently essential that all staff are fully trained in its usage. There may be cultural and behavioral problems with this. For example, those in managerial, professional or technological occupations may be unwilling to admit to shortcomings in this area. If this is the case then:

» either they need to be counseled through this to the point at which they are prepared to admit to training needs;
» or the problem can be surmounted by providing universal and compulsory staff training regardless of present capability;
» or it must be recognized that continuing lack of proficiency is certain to result in shortfalls in quality and volume of performance, and lack of maximized and optimized returns on investment in the technology itself.

The first two are stress reducers; the last is a condition in which stress will be present.

CONCLUSIONS

Information technology, and Web and Internet access, are now more or less universally available and a central part of organization functioning. Problems, and therefore causes of stress, concern:

» perceptions that information systems can be used as a substitute for full management capability and expertise in the areas of communication, information provision, and retention and business planning;
» a lack of understanding of what the communication aspects can be expected to provide and a widespread unwillingness to do anything substantial to address this; and

» a lack of willingness to become proficient (and to insist that everyone who needs to, does so) in the use and application of the technology in particular sets of circumstances, and to understand the environmental and operational pressures and constraints that it may bring.

It is apparent that there are major required features of management expertise if the technology is to be fully exploited and if it is to make an enduring and sustained contribution to business and organization performance. These are also key factors in addressing, managing, and resolving particular problems, stresses, and strains that complex technology brings with it.

BEST PRACTICE CASE STUDY: TESCODIRECT.COM

Tesco Plc. is the largest UK supermarket chain. It has a 21% share of the groceries market in the UK. It has overseas interests in Thailand, where it owns the Lotus chain of supermarkets, and in Poland, Hungary, the Czech Republic, and Slovakia, where it has opened state of the art superstores in major cities in these countries.

Tescodirect.com was opened in October 1998 as a "virtual grocer." The aim was to generate 4% of total turnover via the Website, which could become the company's "virtual branch" – effectively its (at the time) 869th store.

Potential sources of stress quickly became apparent, especially at the point of customer service.

» **Delivery staff**: those ordering their groceries over the Internet were given a three hour window during which their order would be delivered. Ability to meet these deadlines was only partially in the hands of delivery drivers, given the state of traffic on UK roads, and the fact that the majority of customers lived in urban areas. Those who lived in rural areas also suffered because of the long distances involved in some cases. It also became apparent that not every order included the offers and discounts that were available to those who went to the company's stores to do their shopping. Delivery staff therefore found themselves struggling through congested traffic or along country roads, only to be faced with complaints of lateness, overpricing and wrong deliveries. This was accentuated by the fact that because there was very little within their control, there was consequently little that they could do about it to resolve the customer's dissatisfaction.

» **Customer services and public relations staff**: the volume and nature of complaints handled consequently rose sharply. While the company has always adopted a very positive attitude towards complaints based on a "no quibble" replacement and refund policy, the sheer volume of complaints nevertheless caused stress.

The company addressed each as follows.

» Drivers were given small amounts of generic and highly demanded products to carry in the vans so that, where orders were incomplete or inaccurate, there was the potential for putting them right. They were also given discount vouchers that they could issue at their discretion, to actual and perceived aggrieved customers.

» Additional customer services and public relations staff were taken on, and others were trained in this expertise as part of multi-skilling and organization development programs. This was because the company recognized that dealing with extensive volumes of complaints is, in itself, stressful and harmful in the long term to individual general well-being.

After its launch Tescodirect.com had an initial surge of interest followed by a sharp decline in usage. In 2001 it reported that only 15% of customers who had used the Internet service had done so three times or more. Nevertheless, pronouncing itself satisfied with the performance of Tescodirect.com, and with its specific resolution of stress-related problems, it announced a joint venture with Safeway.com to open up the virtual groceries market in the US in June 2001.

KEY LEARNING POINTS

» Recognizing the general quality, value, usefulness, and short-comings of the Internet and electronic information systems; and recognizing these as a source and cause of stress.

» Understanding the problems of information underload and overload.

» Understanding that the fundamental principles of effective management style transcend the e-dimension, and must not be a substitute for it.

» Understanding that e-business brings its own fresh sets of stresses and strains and that these have to be addressed on the basis of understanding rather than assumption.

The Global Dimension

- » Acceptance of stress as a problem
- » Cultural, social, and ethical constraints
- » Managing across cultures
- » Conclusions
- » Best practice casestudy: Oxfam

INTRODUCTION

It is clear that lessons on identifying and managing stress can be learned from anywhere in the world (see Chapter 3). It is also apparent from this that it is a universal problem and therefore certain to be a management and human concern in every sector and location.

The key points are:

» understanding and accepting that there is a problem;
» understanding the cultural, social, and ethical constraints within which activities have to take place; and
» devising managerial and supervisory styles and expertise capable of managing across cultures so that the problems of stress can be addressed and resolved wherever they occur, and whatever the circumstances.

ACCEPTANCE OF STRESS AS A PROBLEM

Barriers to the acceptance of stress as a problem are social, cultural, and prejudicial, and these are compounded by the inability to observe the physical symptoms in the same way as physical illness and injury. These are often reinforced by social, professional, and occupational groups because they themselves do not wish to be perceived as weak or inadequate. Where this is reinforced politically and operationally, the pressure to refuse to address the problem can be overwhelming (see Summary box 5.1).

SUMMARY BOX 5.1: JUNIOR DOCTORS IN THE UK

A junior doctor on his first placement was working at a large city hospital in south-west England. He had worked for 114 of the past 144 hours. Finally, he finished his last round and went to bed.

A short time later his bleeper went off. There was an emergency. He struggled back to the wards. He arrived, carried out the job, and returned to bed.

He was woken some time later by his supervisor who demanded to know why he had gone naked on to the wards. The junior could only stare. He had no knowledge or recollection of having got out of bed, or of the crises or patients. It was only possible to prove to him that he had indeed done so by showing him the notes that he had written up. The doctor was put through disciplinary procedures and exonerated on the grounds of extreme stress.

This situation is commonplace on UK National Health hospital wards. It is allowed to persist through a stated and overt elitism and perceived character strength that means that UK trained doctors can work under any conditions elsewhere. This perception is carefully fueled so that UK public bodies and political interests do not have to pay for better training, more staff or enhanced quality of working life.

The problem can also be quite deliberately misrepresented as an attitudinal or behavioral problem, a lack of motivation, commitment or loyalty. In these cases, organizations transmit the problem to the staff. They are effectively saying: "if you are feeling stress, it is because you are not up to the job," rather than looking at the shortcomings in policies, processes, practices, and management style. In these cases also, it may be possible to sustain an impression of overtly effective performance (see Summary box 5.2).

SUMMARY BOX 5.2: NORDSTROM

At Nordstrom stores, the Seattle-based chain of upscale department stores, live music from grand pianos fills the air, displays are packed with the latest designer fashions, and smiling sales staff walk the marble floors lending the utmost in service to pampered customers.

Behind the scenes there is a different story. Signs admonishing "Don't let us down" and "Be the top pace setter" hang from the walls of the staff rooms. Alongside these are graphs charting each salesperson's hourly performance, complete with red lines distinguishing those who are safe from those who will be sent packing. Because a low sales per hour figure is grounds for dismissal, staff are encouraged to do a lot of their non-sales work out of hours. Restocking shelves, making customer deliveries, going to Saturday morning department meetings, and writing thank you notes are key parts of the job but ones for which they are not paid. Also, to keep up their sales figures, staff do a lot of things to steal customers from each other.

With all this going on, the staff might have little to smile about, but smile they must. To make sure they do, the stores hire secret shoppers who monitor staff demeanor. If they are caught frowning they earn demerits that can lead to termination. As a reward, those who are found smiling the most might win their store's smiling contest, celebrated by having their picture posted on the staff room wall.

If you are going to smile, you have to do it for quite some time for it is not unusual for staff to work 12-15 hour days for well over a week. This is completely consistent with the company's top management belief that many staff do not work hard enough. Indeed, official communications have indicated that even one sick day in three months is considered excessive and indicates a lack of dedication.

These tactics have left some staff with ulcers, colitis, and tremors. In the words of one long time employee: "the girls around me were dropping like flies. Everyone was always in tears. You feel like an absolute nothing working for them."

Another said: "before you know it, your whole life is Nordstrom's. But you can't complain because then your manager would schedule you for the bad hours, your sales per hour would fall, and the next thing you know, you're out of the door." Both these employees, consistently high performers, eventually quit Nordstrom, taking jobs with higher pay and fewer hours - one after developing an ulcer, and the other out of sheer exhaustion.

Now faced with pressure from unions, lawsuits, and lackluster sales, the company is reconsidering its tactics. It is clear that conditions have been improving. It is also clear that without the outside pressure, little would have been done.

Source: Greenberg, J. and Baron, R.A. (1995) *Behavior in Organizations.* Prentice Hall International.

The problems inherent in each of the above cases would be avoided if there were agreement to acknowledge the extreme stress present. It is also certain that organizational, collective, and individual performance would improve if, as the result of acknowledging the stress present, attention were paid to enhancing the quality of working life and supervisory style.

While the problems as presented here may be self-evident, it is much harder to get managers to accept them within organizations in practice. It is very easy to become so embroiled in the pressures of the working, commercial, and operational environment that these come to be accepted as facts of life rather than demands for intervention. The first problem is therefore to get managers and supervisors to recognize the potential for stress and to follow this up with attention to specific indicators. These include the following.

Disciplinary proceedings, grievance and dispute

Attention should be given to the extent, nature, and prevalence of disciplinary proceedings, grievances and disputes, the sources and causes of these, and whether there are high proportions of each in any department, division, function, occupation or location.

Accidents and emergencies

The extent and nature of accidents and emergencies themselves is always a sure sign of low motivation and morale, if not outright stress. However, serious disasters can very often be traced to organization and employee stress factors. For example:

» the pilot of the Singapore Airlines 747 that crashed during take-off at Hong Kong in 1999 had been ordered to do so against his better judgment;

» the driver of the lorry that caused the Mont Blanc fire in France in 1998 had been driving for over 16 hours on the instructions of his company and in breach of tachograph regulations; and

» those responsible for the Bhopal and Seveso chemical disasters had been ordered to meet production targets at the expense of safety.

Absenteeism and staff turnover

The extent and prevalence of absenteeism and turnover again requires investigation into professional, occupational, departmental, divisional, functional, and work performance, and on the basis of location. Reasons for absenteeism can be assessed upon return to work, and, so long as a confidential and non-punitive environment is created in which staff have full confidence, stress-related elements can be brought out and remedial action taken where required.

Turnover may be harder to assess from this point of view but it should be tackled if possible. Properly structured exit interviews produce information and insights into reasons why staff leave particular locations or occupations. Many of these will have a stress element. Even where staff are moving on to greater opportunities at a larger organization or at a better location, it may have been frustration with the present set-up that caused them to look for new jobs in the first place. Especially if trends become apparent, the information can be used to inform management of:

» the real reasons for staff dissatisfaction and why they are moving on;
» specific stress-related elements; and
» derived stress-related elements (e.g. frustration at present lack of variety, enhancement or opportunities).

Organizations and managers can then decide whether it is possible to do anything about this, and whether or not they want to; and if they do want to do something, then it is in response to proper information rather than assumption and preconception.

It may also bring to light specific causes of stress that can, and must, be remedied through management training and development (see Summary box 5.3).

SUMMARY BOX 5.3: SATAN AND BOB

"This incident happened to a former colleague at a bank. Let's call him *Bob*. Bob was assigned an urgent project with very high priority which involved designing a new product in a very short period. Bob worked 18 hour days for weeks. He treated weekends just like weekdays. He only went home to sleep. The project was completed on time and Bob's boss, who we'll call *Satan*, was congratulated heartily by the bank's executives.

The next week was time for Bob's performance review.

The meeting took five minutes. Satan sat Bob down and said: 'Bob, I think you may be a little disappointed with the rating I have given you. Generally speaking, you have been working well. However, there are two problems you have which need to be addressed. First, I have never seen you go a whole day without unbuttoning your shirt and loosening your tie. Second – and this is more important – you have a habit of stretching out at your desk and kicking your shoes off. Frankly, that is offensive. If it weren't for these problems, you would rate a solid competent. As it is, you are scruffy and I'm afraid that means you are rated as developing.'

Bob is now talking with employment agencies."

Source: Adams, S. (1998) *The Joy of Work*. Boxtree Macmillan.

This form of stress is as likely to be based on ignorance and lack of capability as malice. So long as organizations recognize it as a problem to be resolved and as a development need for the specific individual, it is quickly and easily remedied.

However, in many large and complex organizations it is as likely that these kinds of problems will be institutionalized rather than resolved. Labor and industrial relations staff become involved – it is, after all, their reason for being. The problem is therefore fully investigated, opinions and attitudes are hardened and polarized, and slight (or even serious) disagreement is turned into a major issue. This especially occurs where individuals are believed to be recognized and rewarded for solving problems. Stress is caused because individuals who need problems to solve will find and create them, rather than making sure that conditions exist where they cannot arise in the first place.

CULTURAL, SOCIAL, AND ETHICAL CONSTRAINTS

This part of stress management was introduced in Chapter 3. It is important to recognize the extent and prevalence of these constraints. Great stress can be caused, for example, through insufficient attention to prevailing customs and habits, religious beliefs, and strong social and cultural histories and traditions. This requires the following.

» Acknowledging the range of pressures and priorities that exist in the lives of everyone, including health, family, social, ethical, and religious pressures, as well as those related to work. The outcome of this is understanding rather than interference or imposition.

» Acknowledgement of extreme human concerns. This refers to personal crises: serious illness, death, bereavement and divorce, as well as drink and drug problems. The concern is to ensure that organizations give every possible support to people facing these issues so that a productive and profitable relationship is maintained in the long term. Problems related to drug or alcohol use or addiction always fall into the category of legitimate organizational concern. Organizations must set absolute standards of handling and managing these, and give support through rehabilitation where required.

» Confidentiality and integrity in all dealings with staff. This is the cornerstone on which all effective staff relationships are built. Where confidences are not kept or where sensitive personal and occupational information becomes public property, the relationship is tainted and often destroyed. Confidentiality also encourages people to be frank, open, and honest themselves, and this leads to a genuine understanding of issues, and a reduction in stress, much more quickly.

» Support for individuals when either they or the workplace identify problems. This is to ensure that people are not penalized as the result of these pressures and strains. This reinforces the integrity of the relationship between the organization and its staff. Again, it reinforces the point that conditions must be created in which individuals are able to confront issues knowing that help and support are available and that they are not to be penalized.

The traditional or adversarial view of this approach to responsibilities and obligations was that it was soft and unproductive, and diverted attention away from production and output. Organizations could not afford to be "nice" to their employees while there was a job to be done.

To be effective requires organizations either to adopt the point of view of a corporate citizen or perceived good employer, or to accept that there will be stress-related consequences involving disharmony both with staff and the local environment.

Stress is caused to individuals when they are required to participate in something that they know is either not ethical in absolute terms, or else socially or culturally unacceptable in the particular locality. Where the organizations for which they work are sufficiently confident of their absolute position and feel no need to work in harmony with the locality, individual problems caused in this way are usually insurmountable. The following are examples.

» The world's largest oil companies have always had stress-related problems among their staff who have to manage the dumping of effluent in West Africa and south-east Asia.
» South African mining companies always had problems retaining European engineering staff who came to work for them during the apartheid era. These problems were only partially addressed by the collapse of apartheid and the creation of the rainbow nation. While wages for indigenous staff working at the coal, diamond, and gold faces have risen substantially, basic conditions of employment, including safety and job security, have not.

More generally, ethical dilemmas cause stress when it is known, believed or perceived that a wrong view of something is being taken for expedient reasons. These feelings are compounded when everyone knows it but will do nothing about it. Such a point of view may be sustainable in the short to medium term so long as nothing overt or visible goes wrong. Once it is brought out into the open, however, support and faith in the particular policy or venture normally collapses.

MANAGING ACROSS CULTURES

The main lessons in how this should be done are taught by Japanese manufacturing companies in their attitude and approach to setting up operations in the West. In terms of stress management, they substitute one very real potential source of stress – the pressure to conform and do things their way – in return for removing all the others such as job insecurity, low levels of pay, rewards and achievement, lack of opportunities, alienation, and absence of mutual identity and respect. Staff induction, orientation, and job training is high level and continuous. Multiskilling, full flexibility of working, and all-round capability and commitment are required. In return for this, Japanese car, electrical goods (and lately financial services companies also), and other manufacturers provide the best levels of pay and rewards available in their sectors. This, together with job security, trade union recognition, and commitments to retrain and redeploy, rather than lay off or make redundant, has ensured that a largely stress-free environment is created and maintained.

In the UK, US and newly independent States (the former communist bloc), the companies originally made a point of locating in areas of high unemployment. They effectively "came to live in these areas" as corporate citizens, bringing benefits and comfort as well as work and prosperity. This is achieved through extensive and long-term investment that combines respect for local history, customs, and traditions with long-term provision of high quality work, working environment, salaries, and security of employment.

It is important to recognize that the pressure to conform referred to above has brought with it isolated causes of individual stress, and this is symptomatic of the need to pay constant attention to this aspect of management. For example, Nissan UK had to pay compensation to one female employee when the company tried to insist that she turned up for evening and weekend social functions as a condition of employment. So, even the overtly best employers have to be constantly vigilant.

CONCLUSIONS

These lessons apply to all multinational and transnational companies and large, complex, and sophisticated organizations whatever their country of origin. The keys to removing stress and resolving the problems that it causes are in recognizing potential problem areas, and in setting enduring standards of culture, attitude, shared valued, behavior, and performance to which everyone can aspire, and which accommodate and transcend local, cultural, and social pressures.

BEST PRACTICE CASESTUDY: OXFAM

Oxfam is a charitable organization dedicated to alleviating hunger and deprivation wherever these conditions exist. To this end, it sends staff, volunteers, and aid resources to the poorest, most disaster ridden and war-torn parts of the world where it works to:

» alleviate the immediate problems of starvation and disease;
» teach and direct those involved how to rebuild their lives during, and following, war, disaster, and famine; and
» provide expertise in teaching, engineering, agriculture, and construction so that a positive start or restart is made in as many situations as possible.

The organization works in a highly volatile overall environment. It sends staff and volunteers into extremely stressful situations. The specific problems that it has to address include the following.

» **Isolation**: initial isolation of staff and volunteers from their culture, civilization, comforts, and resources. There is also continued physical isolation due to the fact that many Oxfam projects are in remote parts of Africa, Asia, and South America. Physical contact is often only possible by air or as the result of hazardous overland journeys. Isolation also means that food aid, other resources, and additional staff expertise and volunteers invariably do not arrive when scheduled.
» **Threats of violence**: it used to be understood and perceived at least that religious and charity workers would not be harmed during periods of strife and warfare. In reality this is no longer the case. Staff and volunteers from Oxfam and all the large charities, and from Christian and other religious foundations also, now risk their lives should they find themselves in war zones, or caught up in rebellions and insurrections.
» **Feelings of helplessness and powerlessness**: these prevail at times of major crises. Oxfam and the other main charities put in as many resources, staff, and volunteers as possible. However,

those placed in huge refugee camps and famine relief centers express feelings of being overwhelmed by the sheer scale of what they have to face and deal with – and the fact that they are going to fail to a greater or lesser extent.

Accordingly, the organization takes both strategic and operational views of stress management. It runs an extensive induction program for staff and volunteers at the home base, upon arrival in the country of location, and at the particular field site. Volunteers are located initially for periods of no more than three to six months, and whether these are extended or not is a matter of volunteer choice. The organization provides laptop computers and mobile phones as far as it is able, and fresh clothing and some luxuries are brought in on relief and supply flights (even if much of this is actually used as part of the relief effort).

Oxfam bargains, negotiates, and establishes friendly, cooperative, and positive relations with all the political and public authorities in whose domain it is to work. This means, on the organization's own admission, dealing with some of the greediest, most violent and repulsive regimes in the world in order to establish conditions in which its own people are able to work effectively to some extent, and to protect them as far as possible from threats of physical violence. The organization pays bribes to those regimes and officials that demand them. It has carried arms on its relief flights as a condition of being able to fly in the food aid and other relief required. It maintains regular links with local authorities, Western governments, and intelligence sources, and is now much more readily agreeable to remove its staff and volunteers from areas in which they otherwise face physical and increasing mortal danger.

KEY LEARNING POINTS

» The importance of accepting and acknowledging stress as a problem.

» Understanding the cultural pressures on acceptance and denial of stress as a problem.
» Working within cultural, social, and ethical constraints.
» The importance of understanding the standards necessary to manage across cultures.

The State of the Art of Stress Management

- » Collective organizational attitudes
- » Managerial expertise
- » Conclusions

INTRODUCTION

Understanding of the causes and effects of stress at work is sufficiently well advanced for it to be a major organizational and managerial concern. There are in all situations a wide variety of issues and symptoms that require constant and active scrutiny. Direct strategic and operational interventions can be made. Their effectiveness in addressing particular problems, removing and reducing the institutional causes and effects of stress is dependent upon the collective organizational attitudes, specific expertise of individual managers, and the support given for particular stress management activities.

COLLECTIVE ORGANIZATIONAL ATTITUDES

Strategic approaches to the management of stress depend on the collective view initially taken. This can be seen from the following points of view.

Roots in Theory X and Y (McGregor, 1960)[1]

Theory X exists where organizations take the view that their staff have to be bullied, bribed or threatened if any productive work is to be gained from them. This almost prescribes a stressful organization and environment as a precondition of doing anything constructive at all.

Theory Y states that organizations take the view that effective and productive work is dependent on creating conditions in which achievement will then follow; that staff have the need and desire to achieve and gain intrinsic, as well as extrinsic, rewards.

This looks overtly simple. However, it does not tell the full story as witness many overtly high value, highly satisfying, and high achieving organizations, occupations, professions, and individuals – who also experience high levels of stress. The collective attitude is therefore a starting point only. If an adversarial or confrontational approach is taken to staff, stress *will* be present. If a non-adversarial approach is taken, stress *may* nevertheless be present.

This is reinforced by understanding and attending to environmental factors, role and occupation content, and management style.

Change

A major cause of stress is change. This is for two reasons. The change itself may either be collectively or individually desirable, or not; and secondly change means moving from the known, understood, and familiar to the uncertain and unknown. The latter problem is compounded when no clear end is in sight. The protagonists of creating organizations that are in a constant state of change, and therefore flexible and responsive to every market, technological, and occupational development, very often fail to realize that those involved do at least need to be able to see mileposts, signs, and badges of achievement along the way. Otherwise, everything is perceived to be simply chaotic and uncertain and this, in itself, is extremely stressful.

Even where change is known and understood to be desirable, it still causes stress and therefore has to be managed effectively. Stress management requires that the aims and objectives of what is proposed are stated clearly and unambiguously together with dates and deadlines. Collective and individual effects on staff, occupations, work, and behavior patterns have also to be stated. Mechanisms are required in which individual and collective concerns can be addressed and remedied.

This must include addressing wider attitudes and beliefs. The management of change has come to be more or less synonymous with downsizing, resizing, rightsizing, and re-engineering, all of which are perceived to lead to redundancies, job losses, and lay-offs. If this is the case then people need to know. This causes stress, which can then be managed on the basis that people do at least understand the situation. If this is not the case, then this too should be stated clearly so that people's minds are set at rest.

If the organization is not yet sure what the outcomes will be, then stress caused by uncertainty will occur. Organizations and their managers need to understand that staff assume that "no news is bad news," and should take steps to ensure that effective communications are in place on an open and regular basis. As soon as it becomes clear one way or the other, people must be told. This part of stress management can be addressed effectively whatever the circumstances.

Language used must be clear and direct. It is much better to communicate along the lines of: "We will issue an update on Friday even if there is no further news," than: "There are no plans for lay-offs at present." This is universally known and understood to be dishonest.

Communications should be face to face and fully participative, reinforced with written summaries stating what is to happen, to whom, when, where, and why. This attitude and approach provides an excellent basis for the whole of the human side of management. It also acknowledges the legitimate presence of concerns and anxieties, and provides an acceptable open and ethical basis for this part of their management.

Senior managers who deny the value of this approach either work in isolation from their own frontline activities and corporate support functions, or else fail to adopt it because they are afraid that their own feelings will be affronted.

The extent and commitment to this approach also underpins and reinforces the broader corporate approach to respect and value for staff, and the management of stress in particular. As well as delivering precise, honest, and understandable information to those who require it, the prevailing corporate ethic is reinforced.

Rewards and punishments

Another major element of stress management is creating and operating the conditions in which rewards and punishments are issued. In particular, stress is caused as follows.

» When expected and anticipated rewards are not forthcoming. In practice, if it is not possible to deliver what was promised or clearly understood, those individuals concerned must always be notified of the reasons. Wherever possible, alternative rewards are required. If this part of the process is ignored or dealt with dishonestly, stress, anger, and frustration occur. These are compounded where organization resources then have to be used to address grievances and disputes, and when high quality staff find jobs elsewhere.

» When rewards are stated as being available for one set of achievements but issued for others (see Summary box 6.1).

» When punishments are unevenly distributed, especially where they are different for the same offence on the basis of rank, status, location, occupation or position in the hierarchy. Almost universally, junior and frontline staff suffer more for the same offence than senior, managerial, administrative or support staff.

» Where punishments do not fit the offence. Great stress is caused where people are punished for:
  » events outside their control (and one form of this is junior staff job losses as a result of senior management blunders);
  » breaches of rules relating to ordinary common decency and humanity (e.g. going to the toilet or washroom); and
  » minor breaches of dress code.
» Where punishments do not reinforce absolute standards. Bullying, victimization, harassment, and discrimination are revolting acts that are universally reviled, and great stress is caused to those who suffer these. The penalty for each, including e-bullying and e-harassment, where demonstrated or proven, must always be dismissal. Each is overwhelmingly based on misuse and abuse of power and is morally repugnant. A major positive stress management intervention is effected when perpetrators are always dismissed.

Problems are perpetrated and these patterns of behavior are effectively encouraged when alternative action is taken. Common remedies include resisting claims, refusal to acknowledge or investigate, and promoting perpetrators away from the scene of their offence. The affront is compounded when managers use "I must be seen to be impartial" as an excuse for inertia or an alternative to proper action.

SUMMARY BOX 6.1: SIEMENS AG

Siemens AG, the German engineering multinational corporation, sent 10 of its middle management staff on an outward-bound development course. The event was based on a sailing ship and took place in the Fjords of Norway.

Each of the 10 was to be individually assessed for attitude, stamina, durability, courage in the face of adversity and hardship, response to stress, and contribution to the overall effectiveness of the event. The exercise was part of the company's rigorous process of pre-selecting middle managers for development into key corporate positions.

Nine of the ten exhibited all of the required traits, characteristics, attitudes, and behavior. Each was given a uniformly excellent report. The tenth, a man in his late thirties, complained loudly and long of discomfort, seasickness, the futility of the exercise, and the unpleasantness of the environment. He made no contribution. He was accordingly given an inadequate rating by both the instructors and also corporate management development staff who were present to observe the exercise.

Upon return to Germany, three of the "excellent" participants were given immediate postings, and the other six followed over the coming months. The most successful, however, was the complainer. He was given an immediate assistant directorship based at corporate headquarters.

At first the company refused to justify this to anyone. Under pressure from its works council, however, it admitted that the particular individual had already been promised the job. His attendance at the event was a pure formality so that the company could be seen to be fair to everyone.

Managing alienation

Workforce alienation is a key cause of stress (see Chapter 3). Its potential for existence is more or less universal, and it can be managed into, or out of, all situations. The problem of alienation is therefore organizational. It is not a necessary condition of certain types of standardized industrial production activities (see Summary box 6.2).

SUMMARY BOX 6.2: UNIVERSAL ALIENATION

Alienation is the term used to summarize the following feelings.

» **Powerlessness**: the inability to influence work conditions, volume, quality, speed, and direction.
» **Meaninglessness**: the inability to recognize the individual contribution made to the total output.

» **Isolation**: which may be either physical or psychological. Physical isolation may be remoteness of location, or caused by extremes of noise, heat or cold. Psychological factors include psychological distance from supervisors, management, and the rest of the organization.
» **Feelings of low self-esteem and self-worth:** arising from the lack of value placed on staff by the organization and its managers.
» **Loss of identity:** with the organization and its work.
» **Feelings of being trapped:** arising from lack of prospects, variety or advancement for the future; feelings of being stuck in a situation purely for economic gain.
» **General rejection:** based on adversarial, managerial, and supervisory styles.
» **Lack of equality:** of treatment and of opportunity, especially where the organization is known, believed or perceived to differentiate between different types and grades of staff to the benefit of some and detriment of others.

Effective interventions are possible to address each point. The European Union has legislated for the provision of works councils in all organizations of 20 or more staff. A by-product of this is that it is now possible for specific causes of stress to be addressed on a formalized basis. It also creates the conditions by which more general feelings of powerlessness and helplessness can be brought out and addressed.

Conversely, loyalty to profession or occupation rather than to the employing organization is a more or less universal response where alienation is present. In these situations, people say:

» "I am a surgeon," rather than "I work for the National Health Service."
» "I am a journalist," rather than "I work for Reuters."
» "I am a pilot," rather than "I work for QANTAS."

This is to be contrasted with the approach taken by Japanese organizations (see Chapter 5) where it is considered that the basic requirement is for staff to be able to say with pride: "I work for Nissan/Toyota/Sony."

The key quality required of managers is to acknowledge the real and potential alienation present in their own domain, whatever the nature of work, staff or expertise employed. Absence of identity is symptomatic of lack of confidence, faith, and belief in the organization and its activities, and this is both stressful and detrimental to long-term performance.

Managing roles

As stated in Chapter 2, role mismatch causes stress. This applies where the particular roles are over or underloaded, wherever they overlap with others, and where they are not valued, respected or rewarded in terms required and expected by the role or job holder.

Underload

Underload causes stress through boredom and frustration on the part of the job holder. This is the key to understanding factory, production, and service work stress. It also occurs where, for example, teachers deliver the same prescribed syllabus year after year; surgeons are employed to carry out the same operations without opportunity for variety and development; pilots fly the same planes, on the same routes, experiencing the same jetlag, delays and frustrations.

Underload also exists where, however satisfactory the occupation or job may be at present, there is no opportunity for further development or enhancement. A key general condition required is the provision of opportunities for variety, new challenges, and expertise development and improvement.

Overload

Overload exists where either there is too much for one person to do, or where the occupation is in fact dominated by one set of key tasks so that others are either neglected, rushed or ignored. Effective stress management requires job and work restructuring, if necessary supported by the employment of additional staff members so that a better balance, and therefore increased overall quality of work, is achieved.

This problem is compounded when the overload is caused by having to attend to the least preferred tasks to the exclusion or detriment of others, and by having to attend to corporate, institutional or (in public services) political requests, the value of which is either unknown or unappreciated. Effective stress management therefore requires an active understanding of why individuals come into particular occupations and professions, what they expect to gain from them, and the causes of greatest satisfaction and achievement.

Overlap

Overlap occurs where one role interferes with others. This may be at work, for example, where job holders are also union representatives, or where they have a specific project to carry out above and beyond their normal duties. Or it may be a work/non-work clash, for example:

» work demands eating into family and leisure time against the wishes of the family and friends of individuals;
» requests for non-work favors as the result of professional expertise (legal and medical professions have codes of conduct that recognize and limit the pressures that these place); and
» legitimate personal stress caused through having to make a genuine choice (see Summary box 6.3).

SUMMARY BOX 6.3: MAKING CHOICES

For some people, making a genuine, unpressurized choice is extremely stressful. If people are commanded to do something, then the burden of choice is removed. If it is a clear choice between right and wrong, this is also straightforward. Where the choice is genuinely open, then many people have to answer the question: "What do you *want* to do?" They may have little or no real experience of this. Prior choices were always made because of circumstances ("I worked because I needed the money") or because a path or overall pattern could be seen ("I went to college to get qualifications so that I could get a good job").

People get so used to direction and environmental pressures that when these are removed, stress is created. Effective stress management in these circumstances is therefore likely to take the form of mentoring, acting as a sounding board, and counseling so that the individual clarifies his/her own thinking on the particular issues and is guided through them so that an informed choice can be made.

Lack of value and respect

This is a major cause of stress in structured, bureaucratic and hierarchical organizations. It is compounded by knowledge, belief, and perception that those at the frontline are being asked to make product and service delivery efforts for which they will receive little or no recognition if successful, but for which they will be required to accept blame if they fail.

Such attitudes are reinforced by adversarial management styles based on:

» perceived random, punitive or impossible target setting;
» lack of attention to the total quality of the working environment and relations;
» persistent requests to handle the latest management whim or pressure; and
» use of individual influence based on rank and status to gain recognition, a triumph or some other individual PR coup.

In each of these cases, dilution of the primary effort is achieved and this is perceived as reflecting the lack of value placed on the capabilities, expertise, and efforts of those at the frontline.

Burnout

The phenomenon known as "burnout" has come to be identified and understood in recent years, even if many organizations are still unwilling to recognize and accept that it happens in their situation. In summary, it is believed to be caused by a combination of concentrated physical, psychological, and environmental pressures that render individuals no longer able to perform to any capacity at all in their chosen field.

The earliest defined examples of this were "shell shock" and "trench sickness" (see Chapter 3) in which soldiers found themselves unable to function at all because of the physical and psychological strains placed upon them by the incessant bombardments, killing, adversarial leadership style, lack of respect for life, and enduring human deprivation.

Many who failed in this way were simply shot as cowards. They were always condemned by people who had never themselves experienced the intensity and pressure of enduring such conditions.

This holds true today. High profile examples of burnout include:

» Agnetha Falkstog of the pop group Abba, who was burnt out by the demands of the industry itself–touring, recording, performing–and who suffered three ruined relationships as a result; and
» Gerd Muller, the German international footballer and scorer of the record number of goals in international and world cup football competitions. His career collapsed when he could no longer take the pressures of performing on such a high profile stage. He subsequently became an alcoholic and was declared bankrupt.

Burnout is being increasingly widely recognized in high pressure, long hours professions and occupations such as stockbroking, commodities and futures trading, investigative journalism, and in social and healthcare, and education (see Figure 6.1).

MANAGERIAL EXPERTISE

Effective stress management is based on the collective and individual willingness to understand and accept each of these elements as priorities for attention and to connect these with effects on organizational performance, effectiveness, success, and profitability.

Financial aspects

Quite apart from any moral or enlightened imperative, effective stress management is extremely profitable compared with ignoring or institutionalizing the problems. Effective stress management removes major

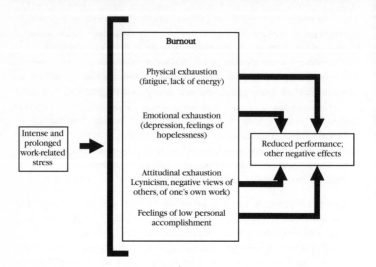

Fig. 6.1 Major components of burnout. **Source**: Greenberg, J. and Baron, R.A. (1995).

causes and volumes of grievance and dispute. Less fixed cost expenditure is required in creating labor and industrial relations support functions to deal with stress. Staff spend a greater proportion of their time at work being productive rather than off sick with stress-related illnesses, or using excuses and alternatives to mask the real problems.

Organizations that take active steps to manage stress are much less likely to face lawsuits, potentially crippling damages, loss of internal and external reputation, and respect. They have greater attraction to potential employees. There is also the belief and perception that organizations which take active and positive steps in the management of stress are much more likely to place higher levels of general respect and value on employees.

Each of these aspects can be clearly quantified. Extensive public relations activities are required and have to be paid for by bad employers to counter the effects of negative reputation. Such employers also have to commit greater resources more often to recruitment advertising, selection processes, sick pay, and support and administrative systems functioning. Those that take an active approach to stress management have to commit resources to training and development of managerial expertise, and organizational and environmental development. However, this is paid for by not having to meet the other demands.

In particular, damages for cases where bullying, victimization, harassment, including sexual harassment, and discrimination are proven are unlimited in the US, Canada, the EU, Australia, and New Zealand. The highest profile cases always attract adverse publicity. This compounds recruitment, retention, and commercial difficulties, and leads to wider loss of reputation and customers.

Human aspects

There is an increasing recognition that those who work in organizations have other legitimate interests away from the place of work. The fact that people do not commit themselves to their work to the exclusion of all else is not, therefore, to be viewed as a lack of commitment or willingness. While individual organizations may take this attitude (see Nordstrom example on page 43), there are nevertheless cultural differences elsewhere. For example:

» **France**: in France there is a collective cultural perception that if people cannot do their jobs effectively in 35–40 hours per week, they are clearly no good at them.
» **Brazil**: Ricardo Semler of Semco takes the view that long-term sustained performance is possible only if people spend time away from work and take proper holidays.
» **EU**: there is legislation in place to ensure that attitudes and responsibilities to, and levels of, parental leave are sufficient to ensure a balance between work and the rest of life.

Managers may view these issues as opportunities or constraints. For example, Fiat, British Airways, Volkswagen and other EU based organizations have chosen to undergo extensive organization development programs to enhance the capabilities and therefore the variety open to staff, rather than viewing social legislation as a cost and burden. In Switzerland, Nestle and Philip Morris have concentrated on increasing productivity and opening up new markets in response to government staff protection legislation. While Switzerland is not a member of the EU, levels of social and employment protection required of employers are very high.

Social and ethical aspects

More generally, it is certain that employers are going to be required to take a much more informed and enlightened view of the effects of stress on those who work for them. This is likely to occur because of:

» ever higher levels of compensation being paid out for stress-related illnesses and injuries; and

» unwillingness of governments and other public bodies to place contracts with known, believed or perceived bad employers.

There are financial rewards to be gained in creating and developing organizations that recognize the potential for stress and take active steps to avoid it.

Management style

Expertise in stress management must be capable of delivery in its environment and context. It therefore requires reinforcement with an overall management style that is capable of recognizing and attending to sources and causes of stress, and willingness to deal with them when they do become apparent. This transcends classical management styles. Effective stress management is equally as possible in autocracies as it is in more participative organizations.

Indeed, enlightened or benevolent despots have always taken the view that their staff are the key to long-term effectiveness, success, and profitability. Julius Caesar never asked his troops to do anything that he was not prepared to do. If they rode, so did he; if they walked, he did so also.

Forest Mars, the founder of Mars Confectionery Inc., made regular inspections and tours of his factories and warehouses to ensure that conditions were good and stress free as far as possible.

These individuals had strong personal, as well as professional and occupational, identity. Stress is much more prevalent in organizations where this strength of identity and cohesion does not exist, and is therefore a likely feature of unconnected, unintegrated role and hierarchical cultures and structures. Those who work in these organizations are much more susceptible to stress-related illnesses, and those who manage in these consequently need much greater overall awareness, understanding, capability, and willingness to address it.

Whether authoritarian, participative or democratic, stress management is certain to be much more effective if managers and supervisors are visible, and therefore physically aware on a regular basis of the activities of their departments, divisions, and functions. Problems are raised earlier, and are therefore easier to address and resolve. Serious problems such as bullying, victimization, harassment, and discrimination are nipped in the bud rather than allowed to fester. Overall, general confidence is also raised, both in this aspect of management and in terms of enhanced mutual respect.

CONCLUSIONS

Stress management is not conducted in isolation. A key part of managerial and supervisory skill and expertise is the ability to recognize and address stress wherever it occurs or becomes apparent. As with every aspect of managerial performance, the quicker stress-related problems are recognized, the less long-term damage is caused to organizations and individual behavior, performance, and output.

The priority lies in accepting and understanding rather than denial. Once this hurdle is jumped, specific attention can then be paid to each of the elements indicated above. Individual and institutional problems can then be addressed and resolved. Each time this is successful, major benefits accrue and these are quantifiable in both financial and human terms. A derived benefit is the development of ever-greater levels of mutuality of interest, confidence, trust, respect, and value, and these are critical elements in ensuring long-term successful and profitable organizational performance.

KEY LEARNING POINTS
» The importance of collective positive organizational attitudes.
» The importance of understanding the specific aspects of change,

rewards and punishment, and alienation as key sources of stress and conflict.

» The financial rewards that accrue as the result of effective stress management.

» The human, behavioral, and ethical rewards that accrue as the result of effective stress management.

NOTE

1 McGregor, D. (1960) *The Human Side of Enterprise*. McGraw Hill.

Stress Management in Practice

» Nike
» Sony
» Broadmoor Hospital (UK)
» Semco

INTRODUCTION

The purpose of each of these case studies is to illustrate how organizations from different sectors and various parts of the world have successfully created the conditions for tackling specific aspects of stress that were potentially present in each of their situations.

The cases are:

» Nike Inc., the US sports, fashion, and leisurewear organization;
» Sony Inc., the Japanese electrical goods manufacturer, and music and entertainment producer;
» Broadmoor Hospital, the UK hospital that treats mental, behavioral, and psychological illness; and which also provides a secure unit for those who have committed crimes as the result of mental, behavioral, and psychological disorders; and
» Semco Inc., the Brazilian white goods and engineering and manufacturing organization.

NIKE: CORPORATE STRESS MANAGEMENT

Introduction

Nike was founded in 1969 by Phil Knight and Bob Bowerman to manufacture and sell sports and leisurewear. The company's first product was running shoes and from there it diversified into a full range of apparel. Originally targeted at the US athletics boom of the mid to late 1970s, the company subsequently diversified into production of all sports goods, initially in the US, and then later around the world. The company now produces a full range of equipment and apparel for football, baseball, basketball, soccer, rugby, and cricket, as well as athletics; and alongside this is a wide range of perceived high quality, premium price leisurewear.

Dividing up the work

Originally the business fundamentals at Nike were organized along functional lines. As the company expanded rapidly this structure began to shift towards product line organization. The apparel and international businesses emerged as separate divisions. Domestic footwear

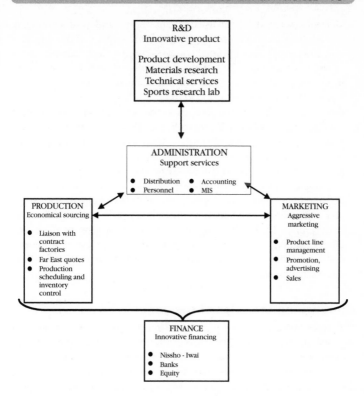

Fig. 7.1 Dividing up the work. **Source**: Christensen, C.R. *et al* (1987).

marketing also became a separate division – product line management (see Figure 7.1).

Pulling things together

As the company grew and jobs were divided into smaller, more manageable and increasingly more specialized chunks, Nike developed three primary mechanisms to pull its business tasks together into a reasonably coherent whole: meetings, defined coordinating roles, and management reports and systems.

» Meetings were the primary communication and problem-solving mechanism. They occurred at all management levels in the organization and ranged from informal conversations to more formal reviews of the product lines. They tended to be scheduled in response to particular needs rather than according to preset cycles.

» Coordinating roles were established to harmonize all activities relating to particular product lines so that one person would assume overall responsibility for research and development, advertising, promotion, selling, and after-sales. This was in response to a lack of understanding of the full strategic approach. For example, one particularly highly motivated sales team successfully promoted a line of footwear in the Far East that was no longer being manufactured.

» Management systems developed piecemeal. The company had particular difficulty in generating a budgeting process. This had to be underpinned by a budgeting, training, and education plan, so that people understood the process rather than treated it as a bureaucratic procedure. It also sought to concentrate the attention of middle managers on managing for profits.

Establishing the rules of the game

The rules were allowed to evolve. The company concentrated on establishing norms and standards rather than written policies and procedures. Some of this had to become more formalized subsequently as the company grew and structures became more complex and diverse. In particular, stress was caused by a perceived lack of fairness and consistency in the operation of human resource and labor relations practices in different divisions and areas.

Providing rewards

For most people, Nike was an exciting place to work, not only at the top but down through the ranks. The company in effect asked people to join a team. People were employed for their contribution, enthusiasm, capabilities, and qualities. Career paths within the company were *ad hoc* and informal. In return, the company took care of people with pay and opportunities for growth, responsibility, and enhanced contribution.

Wages and salaries were considered roughly comparable to those of other employers in the locality; and opportunities similar to those of major competitors – Adidas, Reebok, and Puma. Each employee had their performance appraised once a year. This was directly tied into pay rises and opportunities for promotion and enhancement. There was no organized incentive or performance related pay program. There was accordingly some variation in how well the system worked, and in the equality and fairness with which enhancements were awarded.

Growing larger

As the company grew, management structures and systems became more complex. Growth in sales, products, geographical spread, and employees, together with changes in markets, brought the need for change within the organization. It became apparent to the company that there were three primary areas of concern:

» the continuing need to emphasize the basics;
» the necessity of continuing to talk to each other; and
» the challenge of remaining a team.

The growth, diversification, and increased internationalization of the company brought great potential for stress and were key concerns of the company's top and middle management.

What the company should be

The company sought to return to basics: the goal of maximizing profits. It concentrated on its people, and their personal, professional, and occupational qualities. It established the priorities of innovative products, economical sourcing, aggressive marketing, and innovative financing. It produced "a model for American business – an aggressive, growing American public company." This consisted of putting everybody through a basic retraining and reorientation program (see Table 7.1).

Communication

As the company grew so did communication problems and with these came stresses and strains. It became apparent that Phil Knight,

Table 7.1 Nike: A model for American business – preliminary investigation.

What we were	What we are now
Honest, authentic, fun, dreamers, innovative	Desire to be better but don't know what better means
Small, American, unconventional, never satisfied	Secure about the company, insecure about individual positions
Knew what mattered most – identified problems and opportunities; attacked them without preconceptions or "no can do's"	Too much wishing for a set of 10 commandments – rules and ideas, procedures and practices to make everything easy and straightforward
Made decisions on what could work for us, not on what did or did not work for someone else; used insight, instincts, judgment	Too much refuge in rules or buzzwords when judgment is needed
Run by people who were comfortable with each other and who weren't comfortable in the places that they had come from	Increasing remoteness between different locations, occupations, departments, divisions, and functions
Personal achievement	
Company victory	

the company president, was becoming both remote and insulated from the reality of company activities. The source of stress identified was the perceived ineffectiveness of the vertical line of communication.

It became apparent that the company was becoming too compartmentalized, and that, however good the production, marketing, and sales functions were, a proportion of profit and income was being wasted on the management and administration of a divisionalized structure.

Management development

The company identified the need for developing the next group of middle managers and from these identifying future generations of senior executives and company directors.

Corporate health

Those responsible for the direction of the company recognized the need for the total management of "corporate health." Recognizing the potential for corporate, collective, and individual stresses and strains as the company evolved, the need for management development as a total expertise for the present and future became a priority.

Involvement

The issue of involvement affected all layers of the company. Middle managers expressed worries about the impact of financial success on top management. "How much longer" asked one, "will they continue to work so hard and deal with all the hassles?"

One critical internal observer noted: "We want everybody to be on the Nike team and have the Nike esprit de corps that many of the old-timers feel. But I worry that a lot of employees don't have a clue what it really is."

Another stated: "Unless new employees are capable of assimilating Nike expectations of centered hard work and caring, creative thought, Nike will stagger under the weight of a jet-setting, self-centered, arrogant and average middle management who aggrandize themselves on a past they were not a part of instead of striving for future successes in which they can share."

Finally, another stated: "Each layer is a little more insulated from the rays coming down from the top."

KEY INSIGHTS

» The relationship between organizational growth and the potential for corporate (and therefore collective and individual) stress.
» The identification of key areas where imperfections are present, as the precursor to attacking corporate stress.
» The need to identify specific areas where things are not working as a precursor to tackling corporate and individual stress.
» Hierarchies as potential sources and causes of stress.
» Collective agreement on the main areas to be tackled.
» Concentration on key priorities. If a corporate and strategic

approach to stress management is to be successful and effective, it is essential to concentrate on one or two key areas and priorities rather than becoming too detailed. The key areas and priorities form the basis for a strategic approach to the management of stress; details are handled within the confines of the organizational and management development program.

Sources: www.Nike.com; Nike Annual Report (2000–2001); Harvard Business School.

SONY: THE CREATION OF STRESS-FREE CORPORATE CONDITIONS

Introduction

Sony Inc. began life as the Tokyo telecommunications engineering company. It was founded by Masaru Ibuka and Akio Morita.

The company's founding ideals were:

» the establishment of an ideal factory, dynamic and pleasant, where technical personnel of sincere motivation can exercise their skills to the highest levels;
» the creation of dynamic activities in technology and production for the resurrection of Japan;
» prompt application of highly advanced technology for the good of the general public; and
» the conversion of technical expertise into commercial and profitable products.

Ibuka and Morita also established a philosophy of management.

» Concentration on the long term rather than short-term profiteering.
» Compact size and subdivision of operations through which it would be possible to capture and enhance the profitability of product specialization and market niche concentration, in order to be able to go where larger mass production companies were not.
» Accentuation of the relationship between product and value to society as well as individuals.

» Concentration on the quality of working life of those employed.
» Concentration on enduring product quality and excellence in both established and pioneering areas.

The company started out by trying to commercialize the potential of audio magnetic tape. In the 1950s it diversified into the production of transistor radios; in the 1960s it went into video equipment production (during the course of which it made its notorious decision to produce its own Betamax rather than a generic VHS machine); in the 1970s it diversified into film and music production; in the 1980s it moved into mini and micro cassette, CD, and mini-disc; and in the 1990s it added product portfolio consolidation, television and film production, and computer games and equipment. In the early twenty-first century the company has markets in 146 countries, offering a clear and distinctive brand and perceived quality advantage in music and video entertainment, and electrical and electronic goods.

Building the stress-free environment

At an early stage of the company's development, Morita and Ibuka hired Shigeru Kobayashi as a factory and plant manager. In 1971, Kobayashi became managing director.

Originally brought in to sort out a succession of labor disputes at the company's main production plant at Atsugi, he transformed the whole attitude as follows.

"It was towards the end of 1961, immediately following my takeover at the Atsugi plant, that the following incident occurred. In a meeting of plant management the manager of labor relations reminded us that there had been considerable dishonesty in the handling of time cards. Such cheating could not be tolerated. Watchmen would have to be placed at the time clocks to control the situation."

"I had already given some thought to this time clock problem and hearing this proposal was enough to make up my mind once and for all. 'Let's abolish the time clocks,' I said. 'All they have done is to bring about the war of offense and defense that's now going on between management and labor."

" 'Anyway, what in the world is a time clock? It has nothing to do with the existence of this plant. Our plant is one which produces transistors. To put it in a nutshell, we are being used by the time clock.' "

"So I gathered all the employees together and appealed to them. 'Obviously,' I said, 'we are here to make transistors. Let's decide that beginning tomorrow, we will work according to the time schedule without any clocks. Your own reporting of your absences will be sufficient. The company will trust you.' "[1]

Trust

"When I came to work at the plant I set out to eliminate the complete sense of distrust. This I saw as the root of all our problems. These people had never experienced the joy of living in a climate of universal trust. When management did demonstrate trust, they responded beautifully. You can imagine how exuberant that made us. It was pure joy that we felt, exceeded only by our pride as human beings."

"The establishment of cafeteria service counters without attendants, the improvements made in recreational facilities, the abolition of time clocks and the ensuing changes in organizational patterns were all implemented in parallel. Together, they gathered pace and eliminated the problems almost immediately. As the negative elements in the environment were eliminated, their removal naturally speeded up the progress we were able to make in encouraging people to develop into positive, determined, creative human beings, untroubled by even the slightest feeling of insignificance."

"Once we had managed to create an atmosphere of trust, all signs of discontent disappeared."

"In our plants, we provide orientation for everybody as a matter of course. Like every other aspect of plant management, cleaning is a contributory factor to the production of high quality transistors. Cleaners therefore determine how they can achieve a high degree of cleanliness with fewer people, and what kind of equipment or detergents may be desirable. Every cleaner has their own territory, and territories are rotated. Under this kind of system everybody, not just cleaners, becomes the master of their job and begins to feel that they are their own presidents. The only difference between cleaners and the real company president is that the cleaner sweeps the floors and the president steers the company. Both functions are equally important."

Education and development

"That is not to say that someone should remain a sweeper forever. I am convinced that true education consists in educating the whole person, which includes work. So from an early stage we established a work-study system at our plant. This culminated in the foundation of a Sony Atsugi high school."

"I could not hold back my tears as I stood on the platform during the ceremony that marked the occasion of its official opening. In fact, I was speechless with emotion. What magnificent specimens the students were."

"We at Sony wanted to contribute to the advancement of education on a national basis. For the place of work is a place of education as well. So we needed to provide opportunities and facilities to enable our workers to continue studying as long as they wished. We also had to create jobs that take human beings into consideration and to build an environment throughout every plant in which no job will be despised and all useful work will be respected."

"As managing director, this was my responsibility. Only in this way could I kindle a sense of mission in each of them and make them feel that they had something to live for in their work. Only in this way could I get them to display creativity and cooperation and to ensure that they contributed, not only to their own well-being, but to the development of the company."

Finding dignity and worth

"This philosophy of mine, I want to emphasize, had nothing to do with paternalism. Many intellectuals have heads full of labor regulations and laws, rather than their own thoughts and feelings. The reason why I feel so grateful for being at Sony is that I have been assigned a job here in which I can find dignity and worth, and that I am being paid on that basis. I have been assigned work to which I can devote all I have and from which I am able to derive the supreme reward.''

"We must try our best to give others what we want for ourselves; that is, give them something to live for in their jobs, give them stability from day to day and from year to year. Managers who think that it is their prerogative to let people who are different do jobs which the managers themselves would not like to do have no place at Sony.''

Other guiding principles

In support of the philosophy of the company's founders and top management, Sony instigated the following.

» **Cellular organization**: in which the company and its departments, divisions, and functions were subdivided into small integrated work teams or "cells," which were each given total responsibility for the ways in which work was carried out, subject only to meeting the company requirements.
» **"The joy of work:"** Western production line organization was rejected by the company in favor of an attitude that enabled everybody to become proficient in the full range of tasks required in their own particular cell or function, and which provided opportunities for development.
» **Teamwork and partnership**: this extended into all functions and had the additional benefit of ensuring that the cells regulated themselves, rather than having to rely on time clocks; people would turn up to work on time because their colleagues required it, not because the time clock did.
» **Mutual trust**: reflected in the abolition of the time clocks and other controls to ensure that a fundamental basis of respect and honesty was established.

KEY INSIGHTS

» The distinctive approach and attitude of the company's founding fathers and top management as a precursor to establishing a largely stress-free environment.

» The identification of a distinctive and clear set of principles on which to base managerial activity. In this case, one which concentrates on the removal of normal stresses, strains, and conflict, rather than on having to handle them.
» The illustration of the key positive management tenet of "if you want people to trust you, trust them."
» The need to support and develop management style so that stresses and strains continue to be managed out of the equation.
» The importance and value of human relations and operational integration as elements in a stress-free working environment.

It should also be noted that Morita and Ibuka have both died and that Kobayashi no longer has executive responsibility. In order to maintain the overall philosophy and distinctive quality of working life, it is essential that the next generation of senior managers is developed into the "Sony way of doing things," including maintaining those conditions in which the presence of organizational and occupational stress is kept to a minimum.

This also illustrates the relationship between high, distinctive, and positive qualities of staff management in general as a precursor to the effective management of stress. A key lesson from Sony is the recognition that, while the potential for stress and conflict is endemic, they need not become realities.

BROADMOOR HOSPITAL (UK): INCREMENTAL STEPS IN THE MANAGEMENT OF STRESS

Introduction

Broadmoor Hospital is located at Crowthorne, Berkshire, UK, some 40 miles out of London. It has two functions.

» It provides psychiatric medical care for the community in which it is located.
» It also has a prison/secure hospital wing in which are housed many of the UK's most notorious, psychologically disturbed criminals.

The working environment is extremely stressful. In common with many other medical and Health Service facilities, and the National Prison Service, the hospital has great difficulty in recruiting and retaining key, qualified, capable, expert, and motivated staff. Problems are compounded by having to work in a secure environment. On the prison/secure wing everybody enters and leaves through hospital security, which is opened when they arrive, locked behind them, and then has to be reopened whenever they wish to leave.

Stress-related problems

The hospital management has to deal with two major elements, each of which has the potential for organizational and individual stress and strain:

» developing strategic and operational management practice; and
» developing and improving staff relations.

Developing strategic and operational management practice

Broadmoor Hospital is run as a UK National Health Service hospital trust. Writing at the end of his first period of tenure in May 2000, the trust chairman, Terence Etherton, stated:

"The past year has been extraordinarily busy for staff at all levels. I must begin by paying tribute to them. All, from the very top to the very bottom of the organization, have had to bear heavy workloads, to understand and implement new policies, often working long hours under conditions of great stress. Yet, despite all those pressures, demands, and difficulties, I feel excited and enthusiastic about the future of the hospital as the place for the care of the country's most damaged patients, and one in which our staff can find a sense of personal and professional fulfillment. The new management structure with three new directorates and the central support unit will be critical to the improvement of standards within the hospital. As well as this, the hospital has had to consider and deal with a succession of external initiatives and new policies over the past year. These include the final report of the external management review of the hospital, new security and child visiting directives, and the investigations and report into security at the three UK high security hospitals (the other two being Ashworth and Rampton). The treatment of high risk, personality disordered patients, the provision of social work services at high security hospitals, and the new requirement for ensuring adequate risk controls will also impact upon the hospital. In addition to responding to, and where appropriate, implementing these outside initiatives, time, resources, and effort within the hospital have been devoted to initiatives of our own. I have said publicly how very impressed I am with the range of training opportunities offered by, and within, the hospital. I am particularly proud of the hospital's workshops on working in a culturally sensitive service which all employees in the hospital, including myself, are required to attend."[2]

The hospital also points to the following areas as key factors in the management of stress within this particular environment.

» Improving clinical services in accordance with both statutory and "best practice" requirements. Above all, there is the need to admit patients who are mentally ill and requiring inpatient treatment within units which have "the least restrictive environment appropriate" for their needs. The hospital has a regular waiting list for men, most of whom are at present in prison. The hospital has established two committees – the Health Improvement Program Committee for patients' health, and the Health in the Workplace Committee for staff.
» Improving information. The hospital recognizes that weaknesses in easily available clinical information in a common and usable form inhibit both the day-to-day management of patient care and the monitoring of service quality. The hospital urgently needs an improved clinical information system and is to develop a detailed specification by the end of the year 2001.
» Capability to ensure that clinical decision-making is evidence based. The problem here is that there is little formalized or stated good practice or evidence-based guidelines for mental health services in the UK compared with other specialties. The hospital does its best to follow guidance applicable to all health services, and to adapt this to

its own specific needs and demands. Evidence based guidelines have to date been developed for the management of diabetic patients, and protocols are to be developed to ensure that the prescribing of newer anti-psychotic drugs is based upon good practice and known and understood outcomes.

» Learning from complaints and incidents. A complaints analysis panel has been convened which is to monitor complaints and trends, and check that actions are taken to follow up deficiencies in the hospital's care and procedures. Serious adverse incidents continue to be subject to extensive investigations. Recommendations arising from such inquiries are incorporated into action plans by the hospital's top management team.

Developing staff management

In common with the rest of the UK National Health Service, the hospital has institutionalized difficulties in attracting, recruiting, and retaining top quality staff. To address this the following initiatives are in place.

» The development of labor relations policies to streamline working practices and provide speedier and more effective procedures for the resolution of disputes and grievances. The hospital's disciplinary system has also been the subject of extensive overhaul. This part of the process has been carried out in spite of extensive opposition from the hospital's recognized trade unions – the Prison Officers Association, the Royal College of Nursing, and UNISON (the generic public services trade union).

» Recruitment drives. The hospital has scoured the English-speaking world, as well as other parts, in order to try to provide steady sources of expert, committed, and motivated staff. A successful nursing recruitment campaign is in place in South Africa; introduced in 1999, this continues to provide a major source of effective staff. The hospital has also established some flexibility in pay and rewards, and other terms and conditions of employment. It has been able to develop an extended career structure, including the ability to appoint "nurse consultants" as a career opportunity for those who work within the hospital.

» Streamlined and standardized patterns of working hours and shift systems for nursing staff. The purpose of this has been to ensure that, as far as possible, people work regularized patterns for extended periods of time rather than having to constantly change hours of work within short periods. In other parts of the UK National Health Service it is not unusual for staff to have to work split day-night shifts; Broadmoor has sought to eliminate this as far as possible.

» Implementing a change management and investment plan to the value of $5 million which is concerned with:
  » developing and enhancing facilities, expertise, and treatment available for those patients in the secure unit; and
  » delivering the staff, expertise, and resource levels to provide modern and appropriate mental healthcare and improve patient pathways to the treatment that they require.

Conclusion

The very nature of its activities means that the environment of Broadmoor Hospital is extremely stressful. The potential for this stress to be enhanced, collectively and for individuals, is very great considering the difficulties in recruiting and retaining staff, and the nature of the service that they are then required to deliver.

The hospital has a traditional public service structure and directorate. Potential for stress also exists because, as well as the internal factors indicated above, as a public service institution pressures are exerted on it from time to time by the media and political vested interests.

KEY INSIGHTS

» The importance of recognizing organizations in their environment as a precursor to the identification of the potential for stress.
» The relationship between stress management and the nature of the working environment.
» The relationship between stress management and the employment of specialist staff.

» The position of incremental, strategic change in the alleviation of stress.

» The need for continuous development of the human, strategic, and operational aspects of organizations; and the relationship between this and effective stress management.

» The importance of a steady supply of capable and willing staff in the management of stress.

» The importance of recognizing the attitudes of vested interests (in this case, trade unions and the political interest) in the potential for, and management of, stress.

» The importance of recognizing stress management as a process. Series of actions and initiatives are never ends in themselves.

SEMCO: FULL PARTICIPATION, OPENNESS AND THE LIFE/WORK RELATIONSHIP IN THE MANAGEMENT OF STRESS

When Ricardo Semler took over the Brazilian company Semco from his father, it was a traditional company in every respect with a pyramid structure and a rule for every contingency. Today, factory workers sometimes set their own production quotas and even come in during their own time to meet them – without overtime pay. They help redesign the products they make and formulate the marketing plans. Their managers run the business units with extraordinary freedom, determining business strategy without interference from those at the top. Workers and managers set their own salaries; though everyone else knows what these are since all financial information at Semco is open to all. Workers have unlimited access to the company's books and accounts. To show how serious it is about this, Semco, with the labor unions that represent the workers, developed a course to teach everyone, whatever their job or level of education to date, to read balance sheets and cash flow statements.

The company does not have receptionists, or any other jobs that could possibly be construed as demeaning such as secretaries or personal assistants. The company does not believe in cluttering the payroll with what it refers to as *"ungratifying, dead-end jobs."*

Everyone at Semco, including top managers, fetches guests, stands over photocopiers, sends faxes, types letters, and uses the phone. The company states that it has:

> "stripped away the unnecessary perks and privileges that feed the ego but hurt the balance sheet and distract everyone from the crucial corporate tasks of making, selling, billing, and collecting."

Ricardo Semler goes on:

> "One sales manager sits in the reception area reading the newspaper hour after hour, not even making a pretence of looking busy. Most modern managers would not tolerate it. But when a Semco pump on an oil tanker on the other side of the world fails and millions of gallons of oil are about to spill into the sea, he springs into action. He knows everything there is to know about our pumps and how to fix them."

Ricardo Semler states:

> "That's when he earns his salary. No one cares if he doesn't look busy the rest of the time."

The rewards in involving everyone in these ways have been substantial. The company has turned itself around from being moribund and threatened with bankruptcy, to a position of relative long-term security, chiefly by refusing to squander what it describes as its greatest asset and resource, its people.

Ricardo Semler describes it thus:

> "Semco has grown six-fold despite withering domestic recessions, staggering inflation, and chaotic Brazilian national economic policy. Productivity has increased nearly seven-fold. Profits have risen five-fold. And we have had periods of up to 14 months in which not one worker has left us. We have a backlog of more than 2000 job applications, hundreds from people who say that they would take any job just to be at Semco. In a poll of recent

college graduates conducted by a leading Brazilian magazine, 25% of the men and 13% of the women said Semco was the company at which they most wanted to work.''

"Not long ago, the wife of one of our workers came to see a member of our human resources staff. She was puzzled about her husband's behavior. He was not his usual grumpy, autocratic self. The woman was worried. What, she wondered, were we doing to her husband?''

"We realized that as Semco had changed for the better, he had too.''

Sources: Semler, R. (1993) *Maverick*. Century Business. Mangold, T. (1998) *The Maverick Solution*, BBC.

KEY INSIGHTS

» Staff and worker involvement.
» The provision of effective and adequate knowledge as an aid to stress management.
» The principle of equality and equity.
» Strategic approach of participative management, and its by-product in the effective management of stress.
» The enduring profitability of the approach.
» The relationship between the quality of working life, and the quality of life overall.

NOTES

1 Lessem, R. (1989) *Global Business*. Prentice Hall International.
2 Extract from the chairman's statement in the Broadmoor Annual Report 2000/01.

Key Concepts and Thinkers

GLOSSARY

Acceptance – individual and collective psychological and behavioral relationships with organizational standards and activities.

Alienation – the negative psychological (and physical) outcome of a lack of identity between individuals, groups, and their organization.

Attitude – the psychological, moral, and ethical dispositions adopted by individuals to others and organizations.

Bullying – the relationship that exists between two or more individuals based on the illegitimate use of power by one or more.

Burnout – the result of prolonged exposure to stress; consisting of physical, psychological, and emotional exhaustion.

Conflict – a state of antagonism or "warfare" existing between two or more individuals, groups or departments; conflict may also exist between organizations and different staff groups and their representatives (e.g. trade unions).

Confrontational approach – the attitude adopted by many organizations in labor relations management.

Culture – the amalgam and summary of the ways in which activities are conducted, standards and values adopted, and the patterns of behavior present.

Harassment – unwanted physical or behavioral contact; sexual harassment is unwanted contact or communication of a sexual nature.

Institutionalization – the physical and psychological acceptance of patterns of activities and behavior as normal.

Management development – a series of learning and training events directed at recognizing and managing stressors at places of work.

Organization development – the institutionalization of high quality and integrated learning and development activities, a by-product of which is the reduction of stress levels.

Post traumatic stress disorder – physiological and psychological responses to the after effects of stress, or as the result of being involved in a major crisis, trauma or disaster.

Role conflict – incompatible demands made on individuals by different groups or persons.

Role culture – the establishment of organizational attitudes, values, and norms on the basis of clearly prescribed job descriptions, and rank and hierarchical relationships.

Role overload – extreme demands made on individuals by either their job or one part of it.

Role underload – lack of intrinsic merit or value in particular tasks.

Strain – deviations from normal states of functioning resulting from stressful events.

Stress – patterns of emotional states and physiological reactions occurring in response to demands from within, or outside, organizations.

Stress-related illnesses – other injuries and illnesses brought upon individuals by prolonged exposure to stress.

Theory X/Theory Y – an attempt by D.C. McClelland (1960) to classify extremes of organizational and managerial approaches.

Victimization and discrimination – relationships based on prejudice and the misuse of power, in which individuals are targeted and denigrated because of their gender, sexuality, disability, location, lifestyle or other qualities.

RELATED CONCEPTS AND THINKERS

Conflict

Conflict is a major cause of organizational and occupational stress. The main causes of conflict in organizations include the following.

» Differences between corporate, group, and individual aims and objectives, and the inability of organizations to devise systems and practices in which these can be reconciled and harmonized.

» The status awarded by organizations to their different departments, divisions, functions, groups, and individuals. This is especially a problem where particular groups and individuals are accorded favored and unfavored status, the means by which this is arrived at, and what it means to those concerned.

» Role relationships, especially the following.
   » Senior-subordinate – conflicts of judgment; conflicts based on work output, attitudes, and activities.
   » Functional roles – conflicts between production and sales over quality, volume, and availability of output; between core and support functions; as the result of personality and professional misunderstandings and clashes.

» Individual conflict – in which individuals experience internal conflict between themselves, the work that they are required to carry out, and the ways in which it is expected. This can lead to frustration in terms of the ability to use expertise to the full, and the lack of scope for professional and occupational development and advancement. It is also extremely stressful for individuals to come into conflict with their organization – for example, while grievances and disputes are present.

It is also necessary to address the extent, prevalence, and nature of the particular issues in dispute and the strength of feelings that the parties involved have concerning them. Conflicts also bring their own sources of energy and effective management must address these, as well as the precise issues.

Source: Handy, C.B. (1975; 1997) *Understanding Organizations*. Penguin.

Realpolitik

Realpolitik is the art of survival in a particular organization, occupation or situation. This requires knowledge and understanding of the ways in which everything operates, and of the different pressures and influences that are brought to bear. Above all, all organizations have their own internal politics – the means by which influence and rewards are gained or lost. Individuals and groups have to survive long enough to become successful and effective within their environment. They have to be able to make use of systems, procedures, practices, and support mechanisms. People have therefore to develop their own format for the roles and functions that they carry out in order to maximize their chances of being effective and successful within the working environment. What is normally required is therefore:

» developing approaches based on a combination of role, functions, and personality; adding a personal strand to the occupational and professional;
» developing approaches based on individual influence involving recognizing the nature of the influence of particular individuals;
» developing networks of professional, occupational, personal, and individual contacts and using these as means of gaining fresh insights and approaches to issues and problems;

» developing funds of bargaining chips – equipment, information, resources, and expertise which can be used in trade-offs and for mutual advantage when required;

» developing a clarity of thought around the entire aspect of organization operations and activities. This is based, on the one hand, on what is important, urgent, and of value to whom; and on the other, what facilitates progress and what hinders or blocks it; and

» recognizing what is rewarded and what is not; and what is punished and what is not.

The inability to operate within organizational political systems is extremely stressful. It is also stressful for individuals who bring high absolute standards and codes of conduct with them to their work, and find that they are under pressure to compromise these from time to time.

Source: McAlpine, A. (2000) *The New Machiavelli*. Wiley.

Toxicity

Organizational toxicity and toxic communications exist in organizations that have acquired the equivalent of malady or disease. The concept is akin to the presence of toxins in the human body, or to toxic or poisonous substances in the atmosphere.

Toxic communications demotivate and demoralize staff and dissipate the volume and quality of organizational effort and effectiveness. They arise overwhelmingly from negative views held and perpetrated by the organization and its managers about the staff; and the staff and their representative bodies about the organization.

Symptoms of this include the following.

» **Blame and scapegoats**: in which organizations find individuals to carry the can for corporate failings.

» **Accusation and back-stabbing**: in which individuals are encouraged to make claims and counter-claims (overwhelmingly negative) about colleagues.

» **Departmental feuding**: that normally is the result of lobbying for status, power, influence, and resources.

» **Meddling**: where individuals and groups try to operate outside their legitimate areas of concern and activity.

» **Secrets**: in which information becomes a commodity to be used as a source of influence and as a bargaining chip; toxicity is compounded when this is controlled, edited, filtered, skewed or otherwise corrupted in the interests of one party.

» **Corporate self-deception**: where organizations and their senior managers create their own view of the world and their place within it. This may arise either as the result of the creation of an elite, which quickly comes to believe in its own infallibility, and the organization therefore follows its path whatever it recommends; or where the organization is in decline and, rather than addressing this, it continues to live on its past glories.

Toxicity is extremely stressful and harmful to all those concerned. It compromises absolute standards of behavior and performance. It becomes a negative form of "people culture" in which the key priority of those present is to ensure their own position by constantly denigrating others.

Source: Hall, L. (1996) *Toxic Communications*. McGraw Hill.

Ethics

A key feature of stress management is attention to the ethical standards present and required. It is concerned with human character and conduct, the distinction between right and wrong, and absolute duties, responsibilities, and obligations that exist in all situations. It is based on a combination of distributive justice – the issuing of rewards for contribution to organization goals and values – and ordinary common decency, an absolute judgment on all activities.

At the macro level, there are issues about the role of the organization in society at large. These are largely concerned with addressing the relative virtues and expectations of different parts of society. There are also important issues of international relationships for many organizations.

At the corporate level, ethics is often referred to in terms of corporate social responsibility and corporate citizenship. This requires concentration on the ethical issues facing individual and corporate activities when formulating and implementing strategies.

At the individual level, issues concern behavior, conduct, and actions of individuals and groups within organizations.

The more successfully managers carry out the work, the greater the integrity required. While it is possible to generate short-term results as matters of expediency, long-term survival is assured only through fundamentally acceptable levels of integrity and conduct. Attention therefore is required to the following.

» Common standards of equity, equality, and honesty.
» Relationships between organization standards, the carrying out of performance, and the distribution of rewards.
» Relationships between means and ends.
» Relationships between actions and motives.
» Reconciliation of conflicts of interest.

The first duty is therefore to staff and customers in order to ensure long-term permanence. This occurs only where there exists a fundamental quality of relationships and activities, and where this extends to all dealings with everyone who comes into contact with the organization. From this arises the confidence and ability to conduct activities over extended periods of time. Ethics therefore pervades all aspects of organization activity and performance. The absence of these absolute standards is stressful to both individuals and groups. In some cases, those with technical or professional qualifications may be able to retreat from organizational into professional comfort. In the long term, however, the inability to carry out activities on the basis of honesty and integrity is damaging to those involved.

Source: Sternberg, E. (1995) *Just Business*. Warner.

General Adaptation Syndrome

General Adaptation Syndrome (GAS) offers a healthcare perspective on the identification and management of stress. It was originally defined as "the sick syndrome" whereby those with a variety of diseases had similar signs and symptoms including weight loss, appetite loss, decreased muscular strength, and no ambition. A variety of dissimilar situations, such as arousal, grief, pain, fear, unexpected success or loss of blood, are all capable of producing similar physiological responses. Although people may face quite different stressors, in some respects their bodies respond in predictable fashions.

Three stages are identified: alarm, resistance, and exhaustion.

» Alarm is predominantly initiated and controlled by the sympathetic nervous system and affects organs such as the brain and the heart, and skeletal muscles. These initial effects are prolonged by the simultaneous release of adrenaline and noradrenaline. This is the equivalent of the "fight or flight" factor referred to in Chapter 3. The effects of this stage are ideally short-term responses operating to enable people to cope with, or adapt to, particular stressors that are present at the time. If the situation can be successfully controlled then organ functions return to their normal state. If the stressors remain at, or above, these levels then individuals go into the resistance or adaptation stage.

» Initial response at the resistance stage is to produce hormones that generate increased levels of blood sugar to provide the body with the energy necessary to cope with the effects of the stressors. The amount of adaptation energy is a function of the physical and psychological condition of the individual affected. Every stressor causes the equivalent of wear and tear, both physical and psychological. At this stage, individuals exhibit high levels of activity; and they get many things right and many things wrong. If the individual cannot adapt then they proceed to the stage of exhaustion.

» In exhaustion, the signs of the alarm stage reappear but at a much greater stress level. This leads to stress-related illnesses, when clinical intervention is required to restore the patient's physical and psychological processes. It is essential to be able to identify the major stressors associated with the illness, and then these can be removed or treated.

The process is shown in Figure 8.1.

This clearly indicates the relationship between effective stress management and the medical aspects of stress. At the point at which nursing and medical intervention is required, so is effective stress management on the part of those in organizations. Each of the systems indicated, and the human response, is clearly observable by those in responsible managerial positions.

Source: Selye, H. (1976) *The Stress of Life*. McGraw Hill.

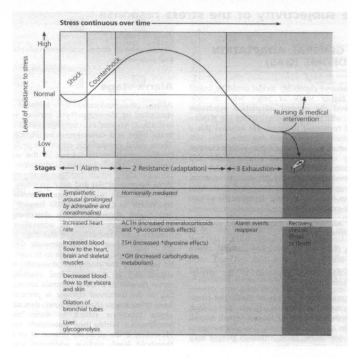

Fig. 8.1   General Adaptation Syndrome (GAS). **Source**: Selye, H. (1976) *The Stress of Life*. McGraw Hill.

Resources

» Cooper, C. & Payne, R. (1995) *Causes, Coping and Consequences of Stress at Work*
» Goldthorpe, J.H. *et al* (1968) *The Affluent Worker*
» Kornhauser, A. (1965) *Mental Health of the Industrial Worker: A Detroit Study*
» Gratton, L. (2000) *Living Strategy*
» Simon, S.B. (1992) *Change Your Life Right Now*
» Owen, H. (1985) *Myth, Transformation and Change*

INTRODUCTION

The authorities summarized below have each produced seminal research, analyses, interpretations, and recommendations on sources, causes, and the management of stress. Each approaches the subject from a distinctive point of view.

The conclusions arrived at, however, are more or less universal. The key is that there are no easy answers or quick fixes. It is essential to understand stress as a medical and psychological condition that requires diagnosis, understanding, and treatment; and to understand the life and work conditions that prevent it or minimize the chances of it arising.

COOPER, C. & PAYNE, R. (1995) CAUSES, COPING AND CONSEQUENCES OF STRESS AT WORK. WILEY

This is an extensively researched academic approach to understanding the causes and effects of stress at work. It identifies the conditions that create the physiological and psychological reactions that, in turn, cause stress-related injuries and illnesses. It tackles the issues from the point of view of:

» blue collar and factory work;
» role, relationships, and responsibilities;
» white collar, administrative, and managerial situations and occupations;
» computer and information technology activities; and
» changing environments.

The relationship between stress and functional activities, especially labor relations, human resource management, and management and supervisory styles; is considered and attention is drawn to the nature of individual and subjective stress responses. The study proposes organizational, managerial, and individual approaches to coping with these reactions. It also draws attention to the critical importance of organizational responses and attitudes to occupational health, and proposes a series of workplace interventions that are available and possible in different conditions.

Contributions to the study come from the US, the UK, Canada, Australia, South Africa, and Germany. What is offered is therefore a comprehensive, substantial, and truly global perspective on the subject.

GOLDTHORPE, J.H. ET AL (1968) THE AFFLUENT WORKER (VOLS. 1–3). CAMBRIDGE UNIVERSITY PRESS

These studies were carried out in the UK in the late 1950s and early 1960s. They came to be known as the "Affluent Worker" studies. There were three companies studied in detail: Vauxhall (GM) cars, La Porte Chemicals, and Skefco Engineering. The stated purpose was to give an account of the attitudes and behavior of a sample of perceived affluent workers – high wage earners at mass or flow production companies – and to attempt to explain them. Both the firms, and the area, were considered highly profitable and prosperous.

The main findings were as follows.

» As far as the job itself was concerned, it was overwhelmingly a means to an end on the part of the workforce, the capability of earning enough to support a good quality of life away from the company. Affluent workers had little or no identity with the place of work or with their colleagues. This was especially true of those doing unskilled jobs.

» Some skilled workers would discuss work issues and problems with colleagues. The unskilled would not. Workforces felt no involvement with the company, their colleagues, or the work. Generally positive attitudes towards the company prevailed, but these were related to the instrumental approaches to employment adopted. The companies were expected both to increase in prosperity and to provide increased wages and standards of living, as well as security of occupation.

» Matters that caused stress, and to which affluent workers were found to be actively hostile, were those concerning supervision. The preferred style of supervision was described as non-intrusive and "hands-off." More active supervision was perceived to be intrusive, and a cause of stress and conflict. Work-study and efficiency drives were also opposed.

» There was a very high degree of trade union membership (87% overall) though few of the affluent workers became actively involved in either national or local union activities. Union membership was perceived as an insurance policy.

» No association was found between job satisfaction and current employment. It was purely a means to an end. The most important relationship in the life of the worker was with the family. Workers did not socialize with each other, either at work or in the community, and the perceived value of the creation of workplace social clubs was therefore diminished.

» The view of the future was also instrumental. There was no aspiration to supervisory positions, either for intrinsic benefits or increased salary. Affluent workers would rather have their own high wages than the status and responsibility – and stress – of being in charge. The future was regarded in terms of increased profitability and prosperity, an expectation that wages would grow, and that standards of living and life would, in consequence, grow with them and remain assured.

These studies illustrated the sources and backgrounds of the attitudes and behavior inherent in this instrumental view of employment. There are clear lessons to be learned about stress management, and about the interventions required by those responsible for the organization and direction of companies.

KORNHAUSER, A. (1965) MENTAL HEALTH OF THE INDUSTRIAL WORKER: A DETROIT STUDY. WILEY

At the same time as the "Affluent Worker" studies were being conducted in the UK, Kornhauser was studying the attitudes, behavior, and lifestyles of car assembly workers in Detroit, Michigan, USA. The results indicated that low-grade repetitive factory work carried out in extremes of noise, dust, and dirt, and managed by an adversarial and confrontational supervisory style, led to both job dissatisfaction and poor mental health. Detroit workers complained of:

» low pay and job insecurity;
» poor working conditions, especially extremes of heat, noise, dust, and dirt;

» low status and a fundamental lack of respect and value exhibited by the company and its managers;
» lack of promotion opportunities;
» the adversarial and confrontational style of supervisors, especially over production quotas, quality of work, and meal and other breaks;
» the extreme effects of scientific management – the simplicity of job operations, repetitiveness, and boredom;
» lack of control or direct input into work; and
» the inability to use other capabilities at the place of work; and
» alienation fueled by feelings of futility, helplessness, and powerlessness.

The stress-related outputs were as follows.

» The workers were anxious and tense, and were hostile to others.
» Long periods of work on car production lines led to negative self-concepts, and reduced feelings of self-worth.
» There was little satisfaction with life outside work, leading to social problems and the extent and prevalence of drink and drug abuse.
» The workers also tended to suffer from personal isolation and despair, and these feelings were transmitted to life outside work.

Kornhauser's studies were carried out in similar occupational circumstances to those of the "Affluent Worker" studies. However, the extent and prevalence of high levels of pay and rewards, and relative perceived job security in the "Affluent Worker" studies, meant that stress levels were found not to be as high as at Detroit. Kornhauser also argued that work with mass production characteristics such as these reduces this pattern of psychological reactions leading to stress, strain, and social problems, as well as workplace alienation.

Much of this was reinforced by a study carried out by R.A. Karasek at the University of Michigan and the Institute of Social Research in Stockholm, Sweden. Two surveys were conducted using random samples of the American and Swedish working populations, and asking similar questions about their experience of work.

Karasek argued that stress was related to two main job characteristics:

» workload; and
» discretion in how to do the work.

Jobs in which workload and discretion are low require little mental or physical activity. Jobs with high workload and discretion are challenging and provide opportunities to develop competence. Jobs with high discretion and low workload may be frustrating and create some stress. Karasek argued that the most stressful jobs were those that combined high workload and low discretion. This argument was confirmed by both the American and Swedish data. Examples of high stress jobs in America included assembly workers, garment stitchers, goods and materials handlers, all those in nursing and hospital activities, and telephone operators.

Karasek concluded that the two main symptoms of stress that could, and should, be observed by managers and supervisors were:

» exhaustion, including problems waking up in the morning and extreme fatigue in the evening; and
» depression, including nervousness, anxiety, and sleeping difficulties.

There was also a strong link demonstrated between high-stress work and the consumption of alcohol, drugs, tranquilizers, and sleeping pills.

Karasek argued that it was not normally stressful to use mental ability, exercise judgment, and make decisions. Stress can therefore be managed and reduced by increasing discretion in how work is performed. Discretion can be altered without changing workload, targets or deadlines, so mental health can be improved without affecting productivity.

References

Karasek, R.A. (1979) "Job demands, job decision latitude and mental strain: implications for job redesign." *Administrative Science Quarterly*, Vol. 24, No. 2.

Huczynski, A. and Buchanan, D. (1998) *Organizational Behavior.* Prentice Hall.

GRATTON, L. (2000) LIVING STRATEGY. FT PEARSON

The approach taken here is to identify the direct relationship between the quality of working life, levels of expertise and commitment,

organization direction, and enduring success, effectiveness, profitability, and viability. Gratton takes the view that once corporate purpose
and priorities are established, a "living strategy" is to be created in
which the conditions that cause stress are recognized and addressed in
advance so that they cannot possibly occur.

The approach is called a "journey." In this, there are steps along
the way – the need for a guiding coalition of directors at the helm,
able to steer effectively only with the active support and identity of
the rest of the staff. Strategic purpose is referred to as "imagining the
future," requiring a human vision rather than one-dimensional aims
and objectives, or something that is purely defined by production and
output targets. The gap between current capability and organizational
requirements – a major cause of workplace pressure, and therefore
stress – is covered from the point of view of recognizing the difficulties
and addressing these in advance, so that the resourcing of performance gaps, problem-solving and organization development become
integrated, rather than separate or dysfunctional.

The accent is consequently on stress recognition, avoidance and
removal from the most positive point of view. Understanding the
universal potential for the existence of stress requires the creation
and maintenance of the conditions in which it is kept to an absolute
minimum.

SIMON, S.B. (1992) CHANGE YOUR LIFE RIGHT NOW. WILEY

The view taken here is that stress is best managed by identifying and
attending to all those aspects of life and work that cause pressures,
blockages, barriers, and dysfunction. Each of these may be physical or
psychological. The approach requires that individual responsibility is
taken for stress management – if the job is bad or stressful then leave;
if the job is good but the organization and management style are poor,
then change employer.

Individuals need to recognize where their priorities lie and adjust
their work and non-work lives accordingly. This is so that the achievement of priorities in the wider context of life is possible. A key part of the
Simon approach is that stress is only manageable when people recognize and understand what they want from life, and take steps to integrate

these elements with each other. They must take active individual responsibility for removing the stressors by identifying the places in life and work where "something has to give." In order to be contented, satisfied, and fulfilled, areas of life and work where people are "stuck" have to be changed, and the consequences managed – whether this affects income, lifestyle, family or social relations.

The book is also very strong on the relationship between organizational, institutional, occupational, and lifestyle change and stress, and especially the sudden perceived comfort of the present that becomes apparent once it is clear that, for whatever reason, change has to take place.

OWEN, H. (1985) MYTH, TRANSFORMATION AND CHANGE. PRENTICE HALL

Owen takes the view that there is great potential for stress in the management of change and the uncertainties of the future. In order to address these issues and smooth the path of change, there is a distinctive role of "myth and ritual" in organizational transformation. Owen argues that:

> "profound change in the environment which requires equally sweeping organizational change cannot be accomplished by tinkering with structure and technology alone. One must look to the depths of an organization that supports the technology and structure in order to facilitate the emergence of new organizational forms."

Myths are the stories of group cultures that describe their beginning, continuance, and ultimate goals. These stories are a key part of institutional and organizational fabric. To know the myths and legends is to know the institution much more deeply than those who simply study balance sheets and organizational charts.

Organizational myths and legends are good stories that create human, interesting, vital, and dynamic views of the world. Working within particular myths and legends is like living within a good story or film. The difference is "you cannot put the myth down. A myth not only reflects life, it becomes life."

Effective stress management is therefore dependent upon understanding the human responses and attitudes to their perceptions of the ways in which the organization functions, and the pattern of feelings, as well as behavior, that they adopt.

Ten Steps to Making Stress Management Work

1 Organizational and environmental analysis
2 Organization acceptance and understanding
3 Cultural issues
4 Serious problems
5 Conflict
6 Labor relations and staff management problems
7 Managing other symptoms
8 Barriers and blockages
9 Repetitive Strain Injury (RSI)
10 Management style and priority

INTRODUCTION

Stress management is substantially about recognizing and understanding the following.

» The universal potential for stress in all human situations including work and organizations.
» The range of sources and causes of stress and pressure.
» The need to respond *either* by taking effective action to address the problems and issues when they arise, and developing the organization, environment, practices, and processes so that these effects are minimized, *or* recognizing the full range of issues in advance and creating the conditions in which stress cannot occur, *or* in which its effects are kept to a minimum.

The following steps are therefore essential.

1. ORGANIZATIONAL AND ENVIRONMENTAL ANALYSIS

Effective organization and environmental analysis depends on a collective and individual willingness to recognize the potential for, and reality of, the existence of stress in all places of work. This means transcending and overcoming collective occupational, professional, and individual prejudices and preconceptions. Once this is achieved, corporate attitudes, patterns of work, inter-group and intra-group relations, and rank, status, and hierarchical structures can be assessed for:

» the likely presence of stress;
» the reality of particular problems; and
» recognizing the drives and restraints, and where necessary, ensuring that the emphasis is given to the drives.

One means of doing this was proposed by Peters and Waterman (1982) (see Figure 10.1).

The approach in the case of stress management is to identify actual and potential problems within each area as follows.

» **Structure**: role conflicts; stresses and conflict based on rank, status, and hierarchy.

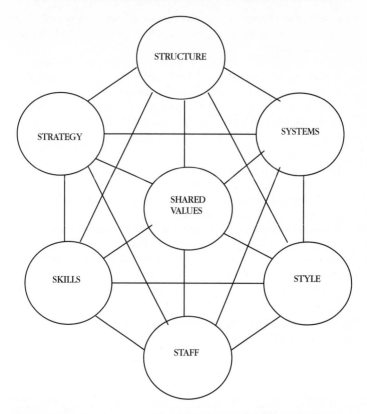

Fig. 10.1 The concept of excellence applied to organizations. Purpose: a configuration of organization, pattern, and design that reflects the essential attributes that must be addressed in the establishment and development of an excellent organization. Source: Peters and Waterman (1982).

» **Systems**: stress caused by the inability of systems, procedures, and processes to make effective operations and activities.
» **Shared values**: the extent to which values are genuinely shared; the extent and prevalence of dissipated and negative elements, including *canteen* cultures.

» **Style**: especial reference to managerial and supervisory styles, and the recognition that stress is caused where these are adversarial and confrontational.
» **Skills**: the requirement of those with professional, occupational, and technological expertise to be able to apply these, and develop these for their own as well as organizational satisfaction.
» **Staff**: general climate of staff relations; particular contributions of labor relations and human resource management.

Stress between each of the elements is likely to affect the following.

» The relationship between strategy and all the other elements, especially the extent to which skills, staff, and systems are capable of producing and delivering what is required; and any blockages that are apparent in structure and style.
» The need to maintain systems for the good of everything else. This is supposed to be a key output of business process re-engineering. However, this in itself is extremely stressful if there is insufficient attention to the human aspects of re-engineering and other restructuring programs.

2. ORGANIZATION ACCEPTANCE AND UNDERSTANDING

This is a key corporate attitude. It is required as a prerequisite of effective stress management. It is founded on:

» understanding the human side of enterprise and activity, as well as the strategic and operational; and
» recognizing the relationship between effective and positive attitudes and behavior, and long-term effectiveness and profitability.

Once this is achieved, specific attention can then be paid to the following aspects.

» Relations between different occupational, professional, and functional groups and individuals where stress arises as the result of known, understood, and perceived differentials in status, influence, and ability to command resources and prioritize demands. Those of lesser influence especially feel frustration and resentment towards those who do command higher levels of influence.

» Working hours, terms, and conditions of employment: especially where these are non-standard (e.g. shift patterns). These bring stresses such as physical pressures caused by long, fragmented, variable or unsocial hours. Attention is especially required to those who have to work variable patterns (e.g. irregular or split days and nights). It is also important to recognize the meaning of "unsocial" in this context. This concerns the difficulty of building any regularized total pattern of life due to constantly varying hours, days, and patterns of work.

» Resource and influence shortages: there is an enduring physical and psychological strain in these situations. It is especially the case that high levels of stress exist among those who know that if something goes wrong there are insufficient resources available to be able to cope effectively.

» Investment appraisal: stress is caused when the behavioral aspects of investments and ventures are not fully considered.

» Constantly having to deal with negative situations and environments: this is an institutional and occupational problem for those concerned with health services management and professional activities; social deprivation and inadequacy (social work and social care); and for those who are employed mainly to handle customer complaints in industrial and commercial sectors.

3. CULTURAL ISSUES

Stress management is concerned with the following.

» Addressing particular cultural and attitudinal concerns that employees have as the result of their knowledge and understanding of the history and traditions of the particular sector, organization, and location in which they work.

» Addressing knowledge and understanding when individuals are to come to work in a new and unfamiliar environment or location. This may be as the result of the following.

  » The takeover of the existing organization by another which has lost its own distinctive and desired ways of doing things. In this case, stress is managed by re-inducting and re-orientating staff into the new required standards as well as operational drives.

» The relocation of individuals to unfamiliar parts of the world. The best organizations provide structured, supported, settling in programs including a set of social, professional, and occupational contacts so that comfort of life and quality of working life are addressed side by side.

Otherwise, general stress management requires that organizations, and their managers, constantly address and reinforce the positive aspects of organization culture, shared values, attitudes, and behavior so that mutual confidence, respect, and value continue to be reinforced and enhanced.

4. SERIOUS PROBLEMS

As stated earlier (see Chapters 3 and 8), key concerns are bullying, victimization, harassment, and discrimination. Apart from the potential for lawsuits, these forms of behavior are destructive to collective morale, morally repugnant, and an abuse of power and position. They cause great damage to those who suffer them. It is essential therefore that organizations have simple, clear procedures for dealing with allegations about such behavior.

It should be clearly understood that false and malicious claims are extremely rare. If they do occur, then the effect is a form of bullying, victimization, harassment, and discrimination in reverse, and the outcome must always be the same wherever proven. *Perpetrators should normally be dismissed.*

It is also essential to protect staff from violence at work, both from colleagues and from customers and clients. This is a serious and escalating problem for those working at the frontline in education, social services, social security, and healthcare. Understanding and recognizing the potential for violence is essential, and this then has to be managed through the use of security guards and systems, and active support for those in vulnerable positions.

Staff in banking, retail, car, and other sales activities also suffer threats and acts of violence from time to time. Organizations have therefore to design premises and the environment so that this threat is minimized. Open premises, such as shops, have security cameras and in many cases security staff.

The presence of security systems is a psychological reinforcement. Where these are not present, staff feel vulnerable to any threat of danger, and this, in itself, is a source of stress.

5. CONFLICT

There is potential for conflict in all human situations. Where conflict does break out, whether formalized in labor relations disputes or *ad hoc* as a part of working life, it is stressful and damaging. Stress is managed when the following actions are taken.

» Developing rules, procedures, and practices to minimize the emergence of conflict, and when it does occur, to minimize its undesirable effects.
» Ensuring that communications are active in minimizing conflict so that disputes are kept to an absolute minimum, and misunderstandings are reduced.
» Separating sources of potential conflict.
» Making arbitration machinery available as a strategy of last resort.
» Using confrontation to try to bring all participants together in an attempt to present them with the consequences of their actions.

It is important to recognize that the working environment and collective attitudes must be capable of dealing with professional and occupational argument, discussion, and debate, while being able to address and remedy the other sources and causes as soon as they arise. Unresolved conflict leads to escalation, and also has stressful side effects such as denigration, bullying, and victimization.

6. LABOR RELATIONS AND STAFF MANAGEMENT PROBLEMS

A key intervention in stress management is the style and approach adopted in labor relations in particular, and staff management in general. It is usual to identify two labor relations' perspectives as follows.

» **Unitary**: based on "the one right way" leadership and management style, so that clear standards are established. These must be capable of overall acceptance and conformity. This brings "pressures to conform" and is stressful to some individuals. The unitary approach comes with active responsibilities for designing, implementing, and supporting clear standards of attitude, behavior, and performance for the good of all. The approach is very successful at Sony and Semco (see Chapter 7).

» **Pluralist**: in which a variety of individual, group, collective, occupational, and professional aims and objectives are accepted. There is great potential for stress and conflict. This is compounded where the organizations are also large, complex, hierarchical, and diverse – for example, multinational and transnational companies and large public sector service bodies.

Such organizations normally have complex human resource and labor relations functions. The primary contribution is to address and resolve problems wherever they arise. The pluralist perspective works best when procedures are designed to ensure a speedy resolution of issues once raised, and this was a key drive of the staff management reforms at Broadmoor Hospital (see Chapter 7). The pluralist perspective suffers in general from being adversarial, confrontational and hierarchical in basic approach, and these are all potential sources of stress. The requirement to employ human resource and labor relations functions is also very expensive for organizations. This has caused many organizations and managers to look at alternatives, and to try to streamline procedures and practices wherever possible.

7. MANAGING OTHER SYMPTOMS

Effective management of the symptoms of stress requires knowledge and understanding of staff, recognition of where the pressures come from, and what individuals do about it. This requires attention to:

» levels of absenteeism and labor turnover;
» location, extent, nature, and prevalence of accidents and injuries, and their causes;
» location, extent, nature, and prevalence of grievances and disputes, and their causes; and
» extent and prevalence of alcohol and drug problems.

In the English-speaking world organizations are increasingly prescribing alcohol-free mealtimes including business and working lunches and dinners (the ability to do this across the southern part of the European Union is very limited). This removes the pressure and opportunity to consume alcohol as part of working life.

When they become apparent, alcohol and drug abuse problems require active management. This normally takes the form of immediate suspension from work, medical examination, and a fully comprehensive and integrated rehabilitation program. Morally, organizations should see employees through the program and back into work before taking decisions on their future. Knowing and understanding that this support is available removes or limits the precise stress of the particular situation. It also means that affected individuals can at least continue to pay their bills while their condition is being sorted out. Above all, it is good for general morale to know that support is forthcoming if employees do get into these kinds of difficulties.

8. BARRIERS AND BLOCKAGES

Barriers and blockages are features of organizational communication. The greater their extent and prevalence, the greater the potential for stress. There is thus a direct relationship between the effectiveness and quality of communications, and reduced stress levels. Barriers and blockages arise either by accident, negligence or design.

» **Accident**: this is where, with the best of intentions, the choice of language, timing or method of communication is wrong. In these cases, those involved will simply step back from the situation and rectify it as quickly as possible. This is the only sure remedy. Stress increases when organizations take on defensive positions and so simple misunderstandings quickly become major sources of dysfunction and stress.

» **Negligence**: this is where barriers and blockages are allowed to arise by default. Organizations and their managers perceive that things are not too bad or going along pretty well. In such cases, communication dysfunctions are seen as "one of those things." Specific problems are ignored or treated with a corporate shrug of the shoulders. From the staff point of view, these are the first signs of corporate malaise and neglect. If allowed to develop, the overwhelming perception on the part of the staff is that their managers and supervisors do not care for them or what happens to them.

» **Design**: this is where barriers and blockages are created and used by those within organizations to further their own ends. They may be used to bar the progress of others. In these cases, information becomes a commodity to be bought and sold, to be corrupted, skewed, and filtered in the pursuit of sectoral interest (see Chapter 9). If not carefully managed, this can become endemic throughout the middle to upper echelons of all public service institutions, multinational corporations, and other multisite organizations with large and complex systems, hierarchies, and procedures.

9. REPETITIVE STRAIN INJURY (RSI)

One part of stress management must address the potential and actual extent and prevalence of injuries and disabilities arising from *physical* stress. The term used is Repetitive Strain Injury (RSI). The key areas which need to be considered are as follows.

» Computer and keyboard working where research strongly indicates that physical stress is caused to the eyes, the back, and the joints in the arms and fingers through extended periods of time in front of a VDU or working at a keyboard (Briner and Hockley, 1994). Workers in the EU are protected by statute which allows a maximum of 2.5 hours working before a break must be taken. Good practice and sound management will insist on this anyway.

» Back injury, which is endemic in nursing, social care for the disabled and elderly, and construction, civil engineering, and other related occupations. It may also be found in warehousing and some other service sectors (e.g. flight crews). The problem is caused by lack of adequate training in the best ways of lifting heavy loads on a regular basis; lack of adequate equipment available when staff need to lift heavy loads; lack of expertise or staff capability to use equipment that is provided. This is a serious problem in nursing and healthcare. It is compounded when there is a lack of managerial insistence that correct procedures and the right equipment are present and must be used.

Organizations in which staff suffer extensive Repetitive Strain Injuries must take active steps to remedy the situation. When there is a failure at corporate and senior management levels to create and enforce adequate procedures and practices underpinned by training and the required equipment, the result will be a high cost for sickness and absence management.

10. MANAGEMENT STYLE AND PRIORITY

Stress management is not considered important enough in many organizations for managers to develop this knowledge, understanding, and expertise. Nor are they encouraged to understand the value and contribution of many of the interventions indicated throughout this work. It is also not taught or covered sufficiently on many business and management courses at universities and colleges.

The consequence is that its effectiveness is uneven and often dependent on the understanding and value placed on it by individual managers. This emphasizes the need for universal coverage. If members of staff in neighboring departments, divisions, and functions receive different quality of attention to stress-related problems, those treated less favorably may complain, take out a grievance or sue. This compounds the volume of stress present overall and helps to spread it across the organization.

Managers must be aware of the benefits that accrue as the result of being a morally high value employer and of the contribution that this makes to profitability and effectiveness in terms of work continuity and commitment.

It is essential for managers to understand and be aware of the life-work balance adopted by individuals within their domain. This means taking an active responsibility, and may include sending people home, as well as insisting that people work in the pursuit of creating an effective, productive, and high-quality working environment.

CONCLUSIONS

As stated in the introduction (Chapter 1), stress brings both financial and human costs. It is clear that effective stress management also carries a range of costs, especially in developing the organizational conditions and managerial expertise required. It is essential that the overall approach is underpinned with positive attitudes and approaches to staff and the capability to manage professional and occupational stress-related problems, issues, illness, and injuries.

The costs involved in creating the environment and in developing the expertise have therefore to be seen as an investment on which returns are expected and anticipated. Put in this way, the returns on investment from effective stress management are:

» reductions in absenteeism, sickness, turnover, injury, and illness;
» enhanced long-term production and effectiveness;
» enhanced levels of commitment and quality of output;
» a major contribution to greater collective quality of working life; and
» a major contribution to collective and individual well-being both inside and outside work.

ADDITIONAL READING

Adair, J. (1986) *Effective Teams*. Routledge.

Ash, M.K. (1982) *On People Management*. Sage.

Biddle, D. & Evenden, C. (1986) *The Human Side of Enterprise*. Fontana.

Clancy, J. & McVicar, A. (1995) *Physiology and Anatomy: A Homeostatic Approach*. Edward Arnold.

Drucker, P.F. (2000) *Management Challenges for the 21st Century*. HarperCollins.

Fontana, D. (1989) *Managing Stress*. Routledge.

Hofstede, G. (1980; 1998) *Cultures' Consequences*. Sage.

Huczynski, A. & Buchanan, D. (1998) *Organizational Behaviour*. Prentice Hall.

Lessem, R.S. (1986) *The Global Business*. Prentice Hall International.

Payne, R. & Cooper, C. (1996) *Stress in Health Professionals*. Wiley.

Pettinger, R. (1996) *Introduction to Organisational Behaviour*. Macmillan.

Statt, D. (1998) *Psychology and the World of Work*. Macmillan.

Vroom, V. (1964; 1984; 1997) *Work and Motivation*. Wiley.

Frequently Asked Questions (FAQs)

Q1: What exactly is stress?

A: See Chapters 2, 8, and 9.

Q2: Stress is one of those things suffered by scroungers, weaklings, and people with no backbone, isn't it?

A: See Chapters 2, 6, and 9.

Q3: Stress was never suffered by people in the "good old days" – why then do people suffer from it now?

A: See Chapters 3, 6, 9, and 10.

Q4: What is the legal position? What are our liabilities? What if we get sued?

A: See Chapters 1, 2, 3, and 6.

Q5: How do we identify real stress? How do we know that the staff are not just having us on?

A: See Chapters 3, 6, 7, and 10.

Q6: How do we create stress-free conditions?

A: See Chapters 6 and 10.

Q7: How do we respond to people who claim that they are stressed?

A: See Chapters 6 and 10.

Q8: What do we need to consider in terms of work patterns and management style?

A: See Chapters 5, 6, 7, and 10.

Q9: How do we deal with bullying, victimization, harassment, and discrimination?

A: See Chapters 6 and 10.

Q10: How much does it all cost?

A: See Chapters 2, 3, and 10.

Index